Matt Damon

Douglas Thompson

First published in Great Britain in 1998
by Chameleon Books
an imprint of
André Deutsch Limited
76 Dean Street
W1V 5HA
www.vci.co.uk

André Deutsch Limited is a VCI plc company

A catalogue record for this book is available from the British Library.

ISBN 0 23399 486 6

Designed by Focus Publishing, Sevenoaks, Kent (Tel: 01732 742456)

Printed in the UK by Butler & Tanner, Somerset and London.

1 2 3 4 5 6 7 8 9 10

Picture research: Lois Linden, Hollywood.
Picture credits:
Hubert Boesl & Kurt Krieger @ Famous
Douglas Thompson Film Archive
Associated Press
Paramount Pictures
20th Century Fox
Miramax Films
Turner Pictures
Columbia Pictures

CHAMELEON

Matt Damon

Matt Damon is New Hollywood aristocracy. Or as Steven Spielberg who directed him in what will become one of the century's landmark movies, *Saving Private Ryan*, explained: '**Matt is the superstar for the millennium. Believe me he is going to play a really important part in Hollywood's future. He's going to do it all.**'

Contents

⭐ Leading Man: Matt leaps into stardom in the multi-award-winning *Good Will Hunting*.

Douglas Thompson

DOUGLAS THOMPSON is a biographer, broadcaster and international journalist who has interviewed most of the world's best-known film and television stars. He is a regular contributor to major newspapers and magazines worldwide. His books, published in a dozen languages, include the television-linked anthology *Hollywood People* and bestselling biographies of Madonna, Clint Eastwood, Michelle Pfeiffer, Dudley Moore, John Travolta, Cilla Black and Leonardo DiCaprio.

For Alexandra

⭐ Golden Boy: shock and surprise as Matt receives the Golden Globe Award for *Good Will Hunting*.

Prologue

Star Turn

'I couldn't have made this more amazing if I'd dreamed it all up.'
Matt Damon
on his stardom, Summer, 1998

HOLLYWOOD, WINTER 1997

There is a moment for all celebrities when they know they have arrived. It is when everyone wants them or their attention. But the most convincing evidence of all is the baying of the paparazzi: for the photographers new stars equal money. They want to see the money, the cash-in-the-bank image, full on, framed in their lenses.

'Matt!! Matt, hey Matt !!! This way Matt, over here Matt!! Just one more Matt? Just one? Come on, just one more!!!!!'

For Matt Damon his superstar baptism happened in a shower of light from a storm of bursting flashbulbs outside the Bruin cinema in Westwood, appropriately enough the university district of Los Angeles.

Damon, young and fresh with a matching smile, couldn't believe the fuss, this clamour for him in December, 1997, as he walked flush and tall in his double-breasted black Armani suit into an altogether different world. It was an early Christmas present, the first of many gifts he had worked for and dreamed about. After all the struggles it was his celluloid *coup d'état*.

As the noise heightened with the banshee shrieking for a glimmer of his perfect teeth, his million dollar smile, his nod – just a look would do – at the Hollywood première of his breakthrough film *Good Will Hunting*, he managed to pull his agent Patrick

Whitesell's arm and stammer: 'It's happening. This is it! Oh, my God, this is it!'

Indeed it was. Only weeks earlier for much of the world he had been 'Matt Who?' Now, he was Matt Damon, superstar. Out of nowhere, it seemed, had surfaced the young actor who was soaring ahead of the 'Frat Pack', his college friends and Hollywood competitors, his peers. He was on the career trajectory of Tom Cruise and Mel Gibson and, echoing their attitude, the young man who still can look like a self-assured teenager was setting his own pace in Tinseltown.

Matt Damon is New Hollywood aristocracy. Or as Steven Spielberg who directed him in what will become one of the century's landmark movies, *Saving Private Ryan*, explained: 'Matt is the superstar for the millennium. Believe me he is going to play a really important part in Hollywood's future. He's going to do it all.'

Good Will Hunting, which Damon wrote and co-starred in with his almost lifelong friend Ben Affleck, opened in American cinemas on Christmas Day, 1997, and the acclaim was instant. The Oscars came later.

Being a great actor has never been the same as being a movie star, an idol to millions. The move from one to the other takes timing and planning – there is rarely anything random about celebrity. Placement of the image is crucial and Damon has been fully aware of his role in his own marketing as a screen star. For this sci-fi fan – as a youngster he saw Star Wars twenty-seven times in its first weeks of release – the buzz was soon with him.

There he was on the cover of one glossy magazine after another and he was Central Casting for the leading man roundabout: tall, trim, with thick wavy hair, killer charisma and a welcoming grin which seemed Pepsodent painted in place. He was a sexy stud whom the camera (still and moving) loved. Nevertheless, at first glance he was yet another Hollywood prince, another product of the starmaking machinery.

The difference with Matt Damon was that he didn't just look good in the role of superstar – he could play it too.

Months later, with the foundations of his stardom fully established he would reconsider the happiness of making it, from looking for work to being able to turn down multi-million dollar offers. With hindsight it doesn't look like a struggle but he admits: 'I wasn't the most gracious person. I'm sure I looked at people, I looked all the time and said: "Why is that guy working when I'm not working?" That's the curse of the struggling actor. A few years ago I would have told you that this should have happened for me then. But I'm glad it happened this way. It does give me more perspective. I'd like to think that, anyway.'

Hollywood was always waiting for Matt Damon. His agent Patrick Whitesell had continually told him so. Whitesell explained: 'This business is driven now by movie stars. More and more the studios need leading men to hang their films on. And once they've gotten past Tom Cruise and Brad Pitt … there's a real need for more leading men. It's a supply-and-demand thing.'

And, he might have said, a luck thing. Damon had been around – and around. He had worked with Chris O'Donnell (Robin in the *Batman* movies) and watched him take on a steady, high-profile career. He and Ben Affleck – and other members of the Frat Pack including Matthew McConnaughey, Joaquin Phoenix, Rory Cochrane and Affleck's brother Casey – went after similar and bigger roles and kept getting smaller ones.

He was a member of a serious but seriously under-employed bunch of talent. He and Affleck – they met when Matt was ten and Ben was eight, united in part

because their mothers were teachers – would talk into the early hours about it, fed-up fighting with their friends for poor parts that other established young stars had passed on. What could they do?

They wrote their own movie, one they both could act in. The idea, grand in design, was to put together a short film that would demonstrate and advertise their great acting abilities. It was a way to increase their odds against all the other pretty boys of Hollywood. Their inspiration was *Rocky*. Sylvester Stallone had written that landmark 1976 movie for himself and against all odds had held out against Hollywood and starred in the Oscar-winning film. More than twenty years later Damon and Affleck found themselves with a similarly hot property.

From a project Damon had created in a university theatre class, the friends wrote the screenplay of *Good Will Hunting* inspired by what they had seen growing up in academic circles in Cambridge, Massachusetts.

Will Hunting is a certifiable genius who is also an orphan whose loyalty to his Boston working-class friends is his life's anchor. He works as a college janitor and amuses himself by working out complex physics formulae that puzzle resident Ph.Ds and talking himself out of petty trouble with the law. In an attempt to channel Will's brilliance into a career, and keep him out of prison, a flamboyant therapist-professor (Oscar-winning Robin Williams) works at his protégé's emotional barriers. Meanwhile, a Harvard student from Britain (the Oscar-nominated Minnie Driver) goes after Will's more personal emotions.

So far, perfect. Will Hunting was a grand showcase role for Damon, the confused egghead's friend Chuckie a solid supporting turn for Affleck. But who had the millions to make a movie of the story the young actors wrote to satisfy themselves? 'My acting agent read it out of a feeling of obligation and probably dread,' says Damon with a smile as he relaxes in the lounge of a hotel in Pasadena, California. The smile is there because of the follow-up: 'Then he called up and said: "You know, I really like this script. I'm gonna show it to our literary department." Four days later they got a bidding war going.'

Castle Rock Entertainment, responsible for some

⭐ **Oscar Boy: with his mother, father and Academy Award to hand.**

major box office films with stars like Cruise, Meg Ryan, Demi Moore, Clint Eastwood and Jack Nicholson, won the first round with an offer of $600,000 dollars for the script. 'It was like we had won the lottery,' said Damon who was excited but not out of control with the deal. Others had offered more than $600,000 but, unlike Castle Rock, none would agree to the clause that the screenplay writers star in the film.

Hollywood being Hollywood it took a year for it all to go wrong. There were disagreements over who would direct the film. Also, the lads wanted actual Boston locations, the would-be producers cheaper, stand-in Canadian locations in and around Toronto.

The complex arrangement with Castle Rock gave Damon and Affleck, who had been making hamburger commercials, thirty days to sell their script elsewhere or the company would assume total artistic control – including replacing the two writers as the stars of the film. 'All that mattered to us was that we were in it,' said Damon. 'We were offered a lot of money, obviously, to bow out and that was something we just weren't interested in doing.

'We were offered a million dollars to walk away. "Look," we were told, "we'll give you anything, just don't be in the movie." But we wrote it to be in it and that was the only thing we wanted. Everybody who bid said they'd pay more if they were free not to cast us but we felt we had nothing to lose.

'I was struggling to make ends meet and Ben was

out of work and sleeping on my couch – he's just broken up with his girl. When the bidding war started we were just spamming it. I mean, it was bad. Within three days they had given us so much money we didn't even know what to do. A lot of the time our mantra was "Sylvester Stallone" because he had done that with Rocky. He stuck to his guns and in more dire straits than we were.'

So did they. Enter Miramax Films – the ground-breaking company responsible for landmark successes like *The English Patient* and *Pulp Fiction* – who paid $800,000 for the movie with the co-writers as stars. And Gus Van Sant, the directors' director, was to be the man at the helm. Van Sant said that he had read only half the script when he telephoned the two writers: 'I said flat out that I had to do it.'

It was an enormous boost. Van Sant had won tremendous performances from River Phoenix in *My Own Private Idaho* in 1994 and three years earlier from Matt Dillon in *Drugstore Cowboy*. Van Sant was – is – one of the most respected of America's 'independent' cinema talents and his reputation for improving everything – including actors' performances – was legendary. Damon said: 'The most important step was giving the script to Gus and saying: "This is your movie now". We had to have a director who was going to heighten it and make it better otherwise the film would have been a total failure for us.'

Damon's share of the loot – at that stage – was one quarter of a million dollars. He and Affleck celebrated with the Frat Pack at a no-frills Hollywood hamburger joint, diet cokes and burgers. Damon and his childhood friend had created their own golden pathway: 'From a very early age we wanted to do this. We've always had a lot in common, similar sensibilities and interests.

'Mostly *Good Will Hunting* is about not wanting regret, about going out and actively engaging in life. "Don't regret what you didn't do. Beat your head against the wall – at least you'll have tried." That's kind of a philosophy that I've always had about acting. I've always felt like, "I'll knock myself out to play this role." I'm somewhat of a control freak; I do everything that's in my power to do the best I can. And if I don't like the final product at least I can say I tried my best. It's just that hard-work-at-all-costs mentality.'

It is a mentality which could have cost him his life. It did damage his health. But it got him noticed and on his way toward the millennium as one of the most sought-after stars of his generation – and the star of one of the most controversial and high-profile films of 1999.

If *Good Will Hunting* brought Hollywood credibility and public admiration, his future roster of movies – working with Oscar-winning directors Steven Spielberg, Francis Ford Coppola (*Godfather*) and Britain's Anthony Minghella (*The English Patient*) – was to put Matt Damon on a pedestal founded on his own determination and talent.

His perfection somehow fits with his pin-up status as the thinking women's leading man. For his millions of fans it's not mind over matter but a combination of the two. His attitude – that much-talked-about deadly charisma – also increases his value in Hollywood. He's got the stardom he's always wanted but is sorry, as a control freak, that he can no longer dictate where it will lead: 'I have to kind of let it go – it's out of my hands now … '

Instead it's in those of Spielberg and Minghella; and in those of Tom Ripley, the macabre creation of the late novelist Patricia Highsmith. This sociopathic and occasionally homicidal character, would change Matt Damon's life all over again. He was going to be a charmer – and a killer.

'We were offered a million dollars to walk away. "Look," we were told, "we'll give you anything, **just don't be in the movie."'**

Chapter 1

The Talented Mr Damon

'He just doesn't feel guilt in a normal way.' Patricia Highsmith on Tom Ripley

ITALY, SUMMER, 1998

By late 1998 Matt Damon was a bona fide international superstar. At airports around the world – Milan, Rome, Venice, Los Angeles, Boston, New York, Naples, Tokyo – he was recognized and photographed.

Following *Good Will Hunting* he had been seen as the star of Francis Coppola's adaptation of John Grisham's bestselling novel *The Rainmaker* and Spielberg's giant World War II movie *Saving Private Ryan*. When he arrived in Italy that year to film *The Talented Mr Ripley* he was astonished to find a crowd waiting for him.

'I thought I was being stalked but they were paparazzi. I couldn't believe it. I just didn't expect that sort of reaction in Europe. Honestly, it's all happened so fast I can't keep up with the attention. I still think it is all hysterical.'

That is something of the anticipated reaction to the 'Ripley movie' which called upon all of Matt Damon's talents and concentration. Tom Ripley is a compelling character – Highsmith chronicled his adventures from introducing him in 1955 in *The Talented Mr Ripley* to *Ripley Under Water* nearly forty years later – but a disquieting one. He is very much a non-hero, a creator of circumstances which feed his own ambition and needs.

Anthony Minghella, with *The English Patient*, had made an award-winning and comparatively popular movie from a difficult novel. With *Ripley* he has surpassed himself. The script remains faithful to Highsmith's novel remains but takes account of the fact that sensibilities have changed dramatically in the four decades since the book was written. With that done the success of the venture rested heavily on the casting – most of all, of course, on who would play Tom Ripley.

Damon's decision to take on the role was a mature one. It was a choice of power over fame, certainly not a conventional career move. This was the actor who auditioned to play Robin in *Batman Forever* and was now being considered and offered the most high-profile scripts in Hollywood. Damon's instincts drove him towards purpose rather than simply Technicolor temptation and into Highsmith's often unnerving world.

Patricia Highsmith wrote about people you wouldn't want to meet. She was a prolific and commercial writer and is a strong seller in high street book shops throughout Europe; and a favourite of the mystery fans of Britain, the audience to whom she is a long-time favourite.

✪ **Poster Boy: moody Matt without the grin, but with extra hair gel.**

'The amount of range required is enormous. **Matt Damon has proved he is a movie star.** What he can do with *Tom Ripley* is proof he is a great movie star.'

Highsmith who was seventy-four when she died of lung cancer in Switzerland in 1995, would, however, be better described as a clever exponent of the psychological thriller. Alfred Hitchcock thought so, turning her *Strangers on a Train*, into his landmark 1951 film. Hitchcock paid her $6,800 dollars for the film rights and it was enough to send her off, footloose, to live in villages in England and France before becoming a permanent US exile in a Swiss valley.

Four years later she published *The Talented Mr Ripley*, which for her coterie of fans worldwide remains a high point and won her the mystery writers' Edgar Allan Poe Award. Her leading man Ripley, one of fiction's more chilling psychos, was first played on screen in 1960 by the young – and, helpful to the plot, beautiful – Alain Delon in director Rene Clement's masterful *Plein Soleil*.

Nearly twenty years later Dennis Hopper appeared as Ripley in Wim Wender's *The American Friend*. Highsmith adored Delon as Ripley and 'accepted' Hopper's 1977 incarnation. Other film versions of her work tended to make her 'cringe'; they were too obvious in plot, usually frank in sexual matters, which Highsmith never was professionally or personally.

Highsmith's style was more subtle, coloured with a fascination with what might happen rather than what actually does occur. Graham Greene called her 'the poet of apprehension' and it

⭐ **Sad-eyed, a young star in character composure.**

remains one of the best descriptions. The novel tells a simple story built up by apparently trivial detail and incident. A young Ripley is asked by a wealthy businessman to leave New York for Rome, locate his son Dickie Greenleaf and convince him to return home. Ripley is smitten by Greenleaf –and his hedonistic lifestyle. He wants them both. Dickie's girlfriend Marge and, as it turns out, Dickie himself become obstacles in Ripley's desires.

Clement created a masterful film: it is against Delon's performance that Damon's will be judged. Even that interpretation had to be reworked into the dominant movie conventions of 1960: crime could not pay and the homosexual implications were toned down.

Decades later Minghella was not censored and, after the 1997 Oscar scoop of *The English Patient*, could do almost as he wished with other people's millions. Leonardo DiCaprio, a global box office superstar with the success of James Cameron's *Titanic*, had been the first casting choice for a Ripley for the millennium, but other young leading men were also mentioned. Matt Damon soon became the front-runner. Highsmith, you feel, would have approved because he has the American 'feel' of how she wrote the young, ambitious Colonial, with an initial lack of sophistication, who would murder in Europe for the lifestyle he aspired to.

Damon's decision to accept was timely. Highsmith's work is resonant again. Ripley, chillingly elegant of intent and mind, arrives in the wake of

The Talented Mr Damon

Hopkins' Hannibal Lecter and Kevin Spacey's erudite, missionary serial killer in *Seven*. With noir again immensely fashionable we seem to have moved on from chainsaws and terminators to cold and calculating protagonists in the Highsmith mould.

Born in Texas, she became a deeply Southern writer, concerned with ordinary people who commit evil; people leading banal, rootless lives, free-floating without religion or family. Maybe it isn't so strange, then that, America has been, and still appears, reluctant to embrace Highsmith and her works. There is a cultural gap in that America, and especially Hollywood, prefers white and black, good and bad guys, with no blurred lines.

But she always saw the extraordinary disguised by the ordinary, the violence and depredation burrowed deep into everyday life – and death which could or might or may be a moment away. Her work revolves around unpitied victims, betrayals and obsessions, and reluctant but enthusiastic murder. Most of that can be found in Ripley's adventures.

Highsmith said of Ripley that he was sane but added: 'He just doesn't feel guilt in the normal way.' The twist – and the difficulty for film-makers like Minghella and leading men like Damon – is that audiences usually root for the intended victim. It's the 'Look Out, Behind You!!!' syndrome beloved by the teen audiences of horror movies.

Damon's job as Ripley was to put audiences – however uneasily – on his side. To cheer the killer, to hope he will escape. Highsmith pulled it off in the novels. As filming began for Matt Damon in August 1998, on locations in Milan, Rome and

Damon's choice to accept was timely. Highsmith's work is resonant again. Ripley, chillingly elegant of intent and mind, arrives in the wake of Hopkins' Hannibal Lecter and Kevin Spacey's erudite, missionary serial killer in *Seven*.

Venice as well as on the Italian Riviera, an impressive version of *The Talented Mr Ripley* was underway.

Audiences meet Damon's Ripley in the New York of 1954 where he is indulging in petty fraud, very small-time, almost-for-fun felonies, and playing piano in nightclubs. Jude Law plays Dickie Greenleaf and Gwyneth Paltrow – the most sought-after leading lady of her generation and by happy happenstance the woman in the life of Damon's best friend Ben Affleck – appears as Marge. The dialogue is always meaningful rather than just clever; Highsmith's eerie perspective always, silently, running.

In Italy, Damon/Ripley befriends and falls in love with Dickie. It is a one-sided obsession that begins to unravel when Ripley is on a beach and totally locked into watching a group of men and boys doing acrobatics. Jude Law's Greenleaf says to him with disgust and disdain: 'I wish you could see

⭐ *School Ties* **with Brendan Fraser are about to be broken.**

yourself sometimes.' It is enough to push Tom Ripley over the edge and Matt Damon into a grown-up world of movie stardom, to separate him forever from the beefcake boys' brigade.

'The casting of Ripley was the most important thing about the movie,' says Anthony Minghella. 'The amount of range required is enormous. Matt Damon has proved he is a movie star. What he can do with Tom Ripley is prove he is a great movie star. I am certain he can.'

Damon may not have Ripley's demons in real life but he shares a sense of deep-seated disappointment with Minghella. The director was unable to become a professional footballer and says of Damon: 'His great sadness in life is that he wasn't tall enough to play professional basketball.'

Chapter 2

Walking Tall

'My ultimate hero is Larry Bird of the Boston Celtics.'

Matt Damon, 1998

Matthew Paige Damon is praised for his good manners and style and much of that comes from his childhood environment in Boston and then Cambridge, Massachusetts. And from his mother, the forthright, opinionated and very non-apple pie Nancy Carlsson-Paige. In the summer of 1998 she remained bemused by his fame, believing it could interfere with the quality of his future life. His mother holds a Sixties' value system; her politics are to the left and very important to her.

It was her feelings and values which would most influence the early life of Matt and his older brother Kyle, who was three when his brother was born in Boston on 8 October 1970. Two years later his father Kent Damon, who was then a stockbroker ('He had a real traditional idea of family life'), and his mother separated but remained close through their sons.

With their father living nearby, the two boys were brought up on Bennington Street in the small township of Newton Corner, which is close to Cambridge, home of Harvard and the Massachusetts Institute of Technology (MIT). Across the Charles River are the refinements and rough areas of Boston. In 1998 Nancy Carlsson-Paige remains a professor of early childhood development at Lesley College in Cambridge.

Her long-time partner Jay Jones, who became a second father to her sons, helped in their progressive upbringing. It included visits to very working-class South Boston, the wrong side of the

tracks. In the mid-1970s Jay Jones had helped 'bus' black children to predominantly white schools in the city. Matt Damon's mother and Jones remained committed to community causes and involvement. When he was twelve they decided to practice what they preached. Jones found a house in the Central Square area of Cambridge which along with some others he converted into a communal housing project for six families. Nancy Carlsson-Paige and her sons moved into the house with its pink aluminium corners on Auburn Street. Kyle Damon remembers:

'About six families bought a broken down house in Central Square and rebuilt. It was governed by a shared philosophy that housing is a basic human right. Every week there was a three hour community meeting and Sundays were workdays. My mom put little masks on me and my brother, gave us crow bars and goggles and we demolished the walls.

'It was nurturing but it was also challenging. There was a lot of love – and talk. Debate, really. We'd discuss everything. It was a great place to people watch, to learn about people – and acting. We didn't rebel much. We didn't do drugs, stay out late or bad mouth our parents.' There were no *Tom and Jerry* cartoons or war games for Nancy Carlsson-Paige's boys. They were given play blocks and, if they wanted something different, the advice: 'Use your imagination.'

✪ **Chris O'Donnell – Matt's casting nemesis.**

Matt Damon was a popular boy. 'He was the guy who sat in the back of the bus always making out with his girlfriends', recalls Casey Affleck, younger brother of Ben Affleck.

← Previous spread

⊛ **Up on the Roof: Matt counsels Brendan Fraser...**

Matt Damon had a lively one and was always conjuring up games and stories, acting out plays. He did his own thing: 'Everyone in the community had their own apartment but the kids felt free to wander from apartment to apartment. This wasn't a communal living nightmare. Everyone had their space and as a kid it was heaven. If your mom was out or not in the mood for you there was always another mother around who was.

'They were hippies. Definitely. They all had the same views on money, politics, raising kids. My mom wrote a book (*Helping Young Children Understand Peace, War and the Nuclear Threat*) about the way kids play with toys. Her theory was that kids' shows were half-hour commercials for products and that companies were starting to tell kids how they should play with toys. So in our house we only had blocks.

'My brother and I hated those effing blocks. What the hell could you do with them? So my brother would make these really amazing costumes which I'd wear and we'd act out these stories. It's when I started to want to be an actor. When *Star Wars* came out we went nuts. We went to see it twenty-seven times, couldn't get enough of it. It was this world of total imagination that was suddenly right there in front of us. I was always acting out these parts and my brother – he went on to be an artist and a sculptor – was always designing these great costumes.

'It seems we were on predetermined paths from a very early time. My parents encouraged us to be imaginative.' But realistic.

His father, who had gone from businessman to teacher and in 1998 was working as a high-school baseball coach, encouraged him in sports. Matt became a basketball fanatic and grew up with the Celtics and the legendary Larry Bird.

His best friend Ben Affleck lived a couple of streets away on Cottage Street. Although two years younger, Ben Affleck was always around the same height – for basketball. 'I played five or six hours a day. In my mind I was going to be a great player. But my Dad sat me down when I was twelve and told me: 'I'm the tallest Damon. I'm 5ft 11ins. Find something else.'

For such a natural athlete – later he would break-dance for money in Harvard Square – it was and remains a great disappointment, but in the giant world of basketball size matters. Immensely.

⊛ **...But keeps his own thoughts buttoned down.**

'Matt and I took acting classes – **I guess you could say we were theatre nerds.** It certainly wasn't as cool as playing on the basketball team.'

Matt Damon stopped growing at 5ft 10ins.

He was outgoing, a character. At an early age he had discussed with his mother the removal from his life of his pacifier 'dummy'. He insisted on throwing it in the rubbish himself and his mother laughs about that memory and, like all mothers, is proud if indiscreet about her son's early days:

'He wore a superhero towel around his neck day in, day out, for a couple of years. I guess he was like a lot of kids – just more determined. He always saw things through; if he made up his mind to do something then that was it. He would take it all the way. I love him dearly but now he's in a world with a totally different value system to me. But let me assure you that's something we can deal with. We've always talked about everything.'

Matt Damon was a popular boy. 'He was the guy who sat in the back of the bus always making out with his girlfriends,' recalls Casey Affleck, younger brother of Ben and part of the trio of actors who grew up at the public high school, Cambridge Rindge and Latin. The Affleck mother Chris was a friend of Matt's mother and a teacher at the school.

But because of age it was Matt and Ben ('He was a charming bastard even then', says Matt) who were best friends. They played Little League baseball together and marathon basketball matches. And chased girls. They also lusted after then young actress Kristy McNichol and Damon says he had a childhood passion for television's original *Charlie's Angels* – Farrah Fawcett, Jaclyn Smith and Kate Jackson. 'We did everything together,' recalled

Matt, whose mother said of the boys who were born coasts apart: 'They were like twins.'

Their environment then – and later – would play an important part in their lives. It was rich with characters and Affleck recalled: 'Where we lived in Central Square you had the working class and the university life – you had to be a lunkhead not to be keenly aware of it. When I met Matt his mom was known as an "activist lefty" teacher. My mom was trying to get me to do more work around the house and would say: "Well, Matt's mom makes him cook once a week." So I first knew him as a guy who was really setting a bad precedent in the neighbourhood.'

They enjoyed 'Dungeons and Dragons', video baseball and watched Godzilla and Kung Fu double feature films at Saturday matinee screenings. On television they followed the adventures of *Super Friends* and *The X-Men*. New Kids on the Block were from the neighbourhood and they admired them until, Affleck said, they realized: 'Joey McIntyre or Jordan Knight could just walk into your shit and steal your lady right in front of you.'

It was a mixed neighbourhood and the two friends were into rap music. They called each other 'Matty D' and 'Biz' and enjoyed their break-dancing. 'Matt and I took acting classes – I guess you could say we were theatre nerds. It certainly wasn't as cool as playing on the basketball team.

'We learned to negotiate and get along with people, be comfortable in almost any social stratum. Friends of mine who had the same parents – a bartender/auto-mechanic/would-be-writer Dad and teacher mom – would probably be considered working class.

'We had our wild times – under-age drinking, pot smoking and the attendant shenanigans. My mother didn't like it but she allowed me and my friends to hang out and drink beer in the basement just so she'd know we were home as opposed to driving around which we probably would have been doing. I became the designated driver for all of us when I turned sixteen and bought a 1977 Toyota Corolla wagon for four hundred dollars.'

Benjamin George Affleck – born 15 August 1972 in the American counter-culture capital of Berkeley, California – was as go-ahead and interested in acting as his friend. His family moved east when he was three and he met Matt Damon five years later. The same year he made an American Public Broadcasting Service (PBS) series *The Voyage of the Mimi*. The educational series about whaling is still screened in schools nearly two decades later. He also had made some television commercials.

Matt Damon was anxious to do the same and worked hard at theatre classes. He won a leading role in a school play – as Humpty-Dumpty. The duo also got work in TV commercials. At school the friends would hold 'business lunches' in the cafeteria to discuss their future acting careers. Ben

had starred in a TV after-school special, *Wanted: The Perfect Guy*, about a son seeking the most suitable partner for his mother, and also had a talent agent in New York. For Matt Damon, striving and hoping for a big-time career, it all seemed a hoop dream.

But it started going beyond make-believe when he made his big-screen debut in *Mystic Pizza*, a 1988 film about three young pizza restaurant waitresses finding love for the first time. Damon had one line ('Mom, do you want my green stuff?') as Steamer, playing the younger brother of Adam Storke. For nearly a decade *Mystic Pizza* was best known as Julia Roberts' breakthrough movie – and now it has become 'Matt Damon's first line movie.' Back then, to Matt and his friends, it didn't seem much of a landmark. But it was enough to spur him on:

'I told my parents: "I'm going professional." They were horrified. But they finally agreed on me going to the city if I used my own money. I went to New York with $200, some money I'd made doing a commercial (a T. J. Maxx advert which Affleck also appeared in), and got an agent. He wasn't very good which, as it turned out, wasn't a bad thing. I had the illusion of being an actor, of being in the business but I didn't get any work so I was doing a lot of high-school stuff.'

'I told my parents: **"I'm going professional."** They were horrified. But they finally agreed on me going to the city if I used my own money. **I went to New York with $200,** some money I'd made doing a commercial and got an agent.'

Walking Tall

At Rindge and Latin, which neighbours Harvard College, the friends met and were taught by Gerry Speca who ran the English and Drama departments. Damon says that Speca became pivotal in his life: 'Outside of my family he has been the biggest and most important influence. He was everything to us – he taught and inspired us.'

Speca improvised acting scenes with his students and would also tape record sequences of action – 'natural acting' – which would be used later to work out 'true' dialogue. People spoke as they did rather than as how they were imagined to talk. Speca was the inspiration for Robin Williams character in *Good Will Hunting*. 'Ben got a lot to do in class because he had so much more experience,' says Damon without any hint of envy.

Damon and Affleck were part of a group which won a Boston Globe theatre award but Affleck recalled later that lessons about acting and Hollywood are altogether different worlds: 'Gerry taught kids self-discipline and to take responsibility for themselves. You can imagine my surprise in Hollywood when I looked around and found that not only is bad behaviour tolerated in many cases it's actually rewarded.'

But for the best friends Speca's methods worked. The teacher says of Damon: 'When Matty was in ninth grade he walked into my class and announced he was going to be an actor. He was a little guy in those days. I still have those images of him running around, rehearsing his part, making sure everything was just right. He was a perfectionist even then.'

As well as playing Humpty Dumpty – Speca says Damon wrote it as an original play based on Italian folk tales – he was in the chorus in a production of *Guys and Dolls*, played a samurai in a Kabuki drama and appeared with classmate Carin Anderson in a school production of Pippin.

Speca, fifty-one in 1998, summarized those early thespian days: 'He was this little dervish, running around, rehearsing his part, all his moves, making sure everything was just right. Big names

have said he works hard and is generous and all these qualities were in evidence when he was a kid. People always wanted to partner up with him. He was very generous.'

Certainly, Speca also inspired the academic as well as the acting bug in Matt Damon. 'I wanted to go to Columbia University in New York and study. In all, I applied to a dozen schools but I think I was afraid to go too far away from home, from my family and what I knew. I got into the local school.'

It wasn't just any school. Harvard is Ivy League and opens more doors than Brooks Brothers suits. 'I buckled down academically because I thought

Harvard would be a good place to start acting. I got the grades to get in because if I'm being obsessive about something I do it.'

He was not so obsessive after he got into Harvard: 'It was so exciting to get in but I didn't do so well when I got there. I screwed up and got a gentleman's B-minus which is basically what they give you when you really should be flunking. They didn't like to acknowledge that they had admitted the wrong person.

'I was just seventeen, just going out and having a good time, playing pool … ' And making films. There was experience acting at the American

⭐ Robin Williams and Matt share a *Good Will* moment of truth.

Repertory Theatre and other Boston-based theatre groups. He says that all he and Ben Affleck talked about was the movies, and acting. In 1988 they did more than talk – they walked on as extras on Kevin Costner's baseball fantasy movie *Field of Dreams*.

Some of the movie was made at Boston's Fenway Park, and Damon and Affleck got to meet Costner's co-stars James Earl Jones and Ray Liotta. It was a proper taste of the big time. But just that –

a taste. It made Matt more determined. 'Matt isn't the kind of person you can count on with dirty dishes but when it comes to acting he is the most focused, disciplined person I know,' says Affleck.

After one year at Harvard that discipline, all the auditions, paid off with a good role in the 1990 TNT cable movie *Rising Son*. Damon played the medical school drop-out son of big Brian Dennehy's redundant factory manager. Piper Laurie, the veteran actress of such landmark films as Paul Newman's *The Hustler*, played his mother. There was serious talent for him to watch and listen to. Laurie, who had played Newman's girlfriend when Newman was Damon's age, says she saw similarities in their passion and style: 'And although they both care about the work so much they don't readily show it. They don't want to reveal just how hard they are trying – it's a sort of shyness. And a pride.'

Not too much pride to try out for any role that looked good, looked a possibility – along with all the other members of the Frat Pack. But then Damon always had the fall back of Harvard: 'After I did *Rising Son* and went back to school I really dug it. Where else can you relax and study Japanese

winning – and Robin Williams starring – *Dead Poets Society*. Ben Affleck was in too and other familiar names from their crowd: Chris O'Donnell, Randall Batinkoff, Cole Hauser and Brendan Fraser.

Fraser starred as a Jewish boy at a New England prep school – the movie was filmed near Damon's home town at Middlesex School in Concord – who is baited and resented by bigoted 'legacy' student Matt Damon. Damon was the most featured of the young players – but it didn't help him when he learned a lesson about the competitive world he was in.

While these members of the Frat Pack were at work on *School Ties* the casting was going on for a major role in a major film. Al Pacino was to star in *Scent of a Woman* as an embittered, blinded Army officer who enlists a young student to show him around, take him on one last fling. It was a perfect role for Pacino – he would win the Best Actor Oscar for it – and a starmaking chance for whoever played alongside him.

'It was everybody … *Scent of a Woman* happened right during *School Ties* and the whole cast went to audition for it,' recalled Damon, offering more detail. 'Chris O'Donnell was a business major

'I was just seventeen, **just going out and having a good time**, playing pool … And making films.'

culture? Each year I kept doing better and better because I realized how great it was to be in school, how it gave me a kind of freedom that I may never have again in my whole life.'

He persevered with acting. He auditioned more than a dozen times for School Ties which every young actor aged between sixteen and twenty-two wanted to be in. Matt Damon made the cut for the 1992 film which echoed the award-

at Boston College and he's a very savvy business-man. So the way I found out about the part is I'm checking in with my agent to see if anything good has come in and my agent says: "Here's one with a young role and … oh, my God, it's got Al Pacino in it." So I go up to Chris and I say: "Have you heard about this movie?" and he says: "Yeah."

'So I say: "Do you have the script?" He says: "Yeah?" I say: "Can I see it?" He says: "No – I kinda

☆ **Matt sips a brew with Ben and Casey Affleck in** *Good Will Hunting.*

need it." Chris wouldn't give it to anybody. Later, Ben, me, Randall, Brendan, Anthony Rapp – we're all commiserating about our auditions, talking about how they didn't go well. Except for Chris. Chris used to play things close to his vest. We asked him how his audition had gone and he just said: "Oh, Oh, it was all right." And we were like: "Dude! Just tell us how it went." And he would say: "Ohhhh, I don't know." '

O'Donnell knew. They all knew. *Scent of a Woman* established him as a major name. Such a name that when he was offered the part of the Boy Wonder in *Batman Forever* he asked for more money. The producers were sniffy about that and put the role of Robin out for auditions. Enter all the lads again, including Matt Damon, who did a screen test for it. But it was O'Donnell who ran beside first Val Kilmer in *Batman Forever* and George Clooney in *Batman and Robin*.

Things could have been so different in a Hollywood moment. Damon may have been disenchanted with his luck but he was not destroyed by it. There were other good roles and some great ones to go after. One of the latter was in *Primal Fear* as an altar boy being defended by Richard Gere for the brutal murder of a bishop. It won Edward Norton an Oscar nomination and made his career. 'It more or less came down to him or me,' says Damon matter of factly.

For Gus Van Sant's dark satire *To Die For* (Nicole Kidman will do anything to further a television career) he went on a stringent diet for the role of the lethal Kidman's teenaged accomplice-boyfriend. But losing nearly twenty pounds in weight wasn't enough. The part went to Joaquin Phoenix. Known as 'Wock' to Damon and the gang, he is the brother of tragic River Phoenix, whose sudden drug-related death on the morning of Hallowe'en 1993 had especially shocked Damon and his friends won that part.

Damon was happy for his friend but then he was used to rejection. He had always been told it had been part of the job. Ben Affleck's mother had

told him every time he went to her house for dinner: 'Study to be a doctor – you can call the shots then.' But he and Ben Affleck had promised each other to take their ambition 'all the way'. That meant Out West, to Los Angeles, where they could be ready for auditions as soon as they heard about them. Their lives revolved around Tinseltown casting gossip and reading the *Hollywood Reporter* and *Daily Variety* with their morning coffee.

Home was a two-bedroom flat – often with other guests – on Curzon Avenue in West Hollywood where Damon played video games and ate chocolate biscuits. 'There was a lot of struggling for us, lots of low lows and high highs. There was five years of that, a long time.' They watched Chris O'Donnell's career take off and Matthew McConnaughey make it in the film version of John Grisham's *A Time to Kill*.

⭐ **Serious superstar stalks the courtroom.**

Damon recalled: 'We used to fool around in Los Angeles together. We always used to say: "Hey, I read this script, maybe we can all do it." We were struggling. There was Ben and his brother and me and Rory Cochrane and Wock Phoenix. We were all struggling. I remember when we heard Matthew got offered a million bucks for *A Time To Kill*. We were all jumping around, screaming. I mean, the fact that one of us was "the guy" was just too much to be believed. We all went nuts. It was such a feeling of vindication that one of our peer group, someone not on the A-list, got the part.'

Matt Damon got offers – but he didn't take just anything. Oscar-driven, Westerns rode back into Hollywood on the back of Kevin Costner's *Dances With Wolves* and Clint Eastwood's *Unforgiven*. Sharon Stone, who with *Basic Instinct*

'It more or less came down to him or me,' says Damon, matter of factly.

had become Hollywood's most sensational leading lady, saw a trend and decided that she should co-produce a Western with herself as the starring protagonist. But as she, and later Damon would find out, even Oscars could not guarantee continued box office success of the genre. In 1992 Carolco had planned to pay the then number-one movie lady, 'Pretty Woman' Julia Roberts, $7 million for a similar adventure movie called *The Revengers*. Stone was now getting the same sort of money – plus percentage profit 'points'.

The Quick and the Dead was backed by Tri-Star Pictures, the distributors of *Basic Instinct*. Stone was working with people she knew. It was anticipated as one of the major blockbuster films of 1994–95. Stone saw that instantly and went into her control mode and Damon was offered one of the most important roles in the film. It was about a tough Wild West woman out to revenge the death of her father, a story packed with a motley assortment of characters with names like Fly, Flatnose, Ratsy, Ace, The Kid and Herod.

Matt Damon could. He was offered the role of The Kid, the Oedipal gunslinger who duels with his father, Gene Hackman – hot from his Best Supporting Actor Oscar from *Unforgiven* – as Herod. Damon didn't like the script. It was Leonardo DiCaprio who got to kiss Sharon Stone and face Hackman in a shoot-out.

Strange as it seems with hindsight, post-*Titanic*, Matt Damon still believes he made the right decision: 'I remember telling my agents: "You know what I did last night? I watched a film from 1968,

Steve McQueen in *Bullitt*. In the film Robert Duvall drives a cab and he has, like, four lines but he was totally believable and really good. At the end of the day he was in *Bullitt*. He's in all these great movies because he doesn't do this kind of thing." '

Had Gerry Speca's values about determination and doing what you feel is right got through? Or was it Nancy Carlsson-Paige's influence showing? Wherever they came from they were clearly part of Matt Damon. And he still got to make a Western and star with Gene Hackman.

Matt Damon remains a most self-effacing star. There's still that gee-whiz factor about him but there is more than hope and chance about what he has achieved. He sat down one morning in Beverly Hills and over coffee and cigarettes showed that rarely seen side of him. He said he had thought deeply and seriously about his chances, the reality of Hollywood: 'I'm part of this cynical generation but the one thing we have going for us is we have a lot of energy. We're willing to run into the brick walls until somebody opens a door for us. When I went to work at becoming an actor I was cynical but I had hope, you know, I had hope that it would work.

'I always felt that some day I'd have a shot. For a long time I couldn't get arrested. You have a lot of young people in Los Angeles who have this feeling of self-worth and nobody to kind of affirm it. And you have all this energy that's kind of unharnessed, a lot of people who want to do it and very few slots that are open to them. It is daunting but, you know, I was always convinced that given the chance I could make it work.'

He always talks about *The Usual Suspects* and the appearance of Benicio Del Toro in the line-up with stars Gabriel Byrne and Kevin Spacey. Del Toro doesn't last long in the cult movie but makes a solid impression. Damon was bowled over by it: 'He's killed early in the movie and he probably has about nine lines but I found it the most memorable performance of 1995. The guy just goes out and thinks: "No one's gonna understand what I'm doing except me but I'm an effing genius … " '

Chapter 3

Geronimo!

'I was sick of reading scripts that Chris O'Donnell had passed on.'

Matt Damon explaining risking his health to be noticed in his role in *Courage Under Fire*

Curzon Avenue, Hollywood, was not the top end of town and not at any glance a MENSA membership headquarters. Matt Damon's buddies including Ben Affleck didn't feel like geniuses – they had found roles in the 1993 movie *Dazed and Confused* and that rather summed up all their circumstances. But there was some word around town about Damon.

His picture had appeared in some teen magazines and his striking features – strong and glowing like his mother's – had turned him into something like a cult heart-throb. At their flat his friends would pin up the pictures and throw darts at them. 'I'd pull it down and another picture would go up,' laughed Damon who auditioned for a movie which – like Sharon Stone's *The Quick and the Dead* – was hoping the Western was not dead.

Geronimo: An American Legend was the work of Hollywood legend John Milius. He wrote the screenplay from his own story and director Walter Hill, himself a cult figure for movies like *48 Hours*, was to direct. The cast was impressive including Jason Patric, who would later take over from Keanu Reeves in *Speed 2* with Sandra Bullock, and in 1993 it seemed a perfect chance.

It also meant working with Robert Duvall, as well as Hackman and Wes Studi in the title role. Damon was Lieutenant Britton Davis, an inexperienced young army officer who gets caught up in the obsessive movement to capture the Apache warlord. Damon's fledgling soldier also narrates much of the adventure. It was a worthy $35 million dollar investment which won critical praise but it was no blockbuster, no breakthrough for its young hopeful in the cast. Nevertheless, Damon felt fulfilled: 'I find that being around somebody like him and just watching them work is the best. I felt that to be in Robert Duvall's presence is like going to acting school, to the best acting school there is.

'I look at acting, writing and directing as a trade, pure and simple. The best way to get good at something is to apprentice yourself to the masters and be properly subjugated – please just let me sit and watch and listen and learn. It is how you learn best.'

Duvall and Hackman were certainly impressed by his devotion, telling him they would happily work with him again – and soon. But it was Tommy Lee Jones, Duvall's co-star from the impressive television epic *Lonesome Dove*, who grabbed Damon's services first. The Texan actor is a taciturn man and a well-connected one; a close friend from college days is the American vice-president, Al Gore. He had been one of Damon's

✪ **A little hair on the upper lip for the more manly, mature look, in the hunt for *Geronimo*.**

Geronimo!

'"I'm making the best movie I've ever made – possibly the best movie that's ever been made in the history of the media." **And adds: "Then it turns out to be a howling pooch."'**

heroes, an actor at ease in all mediums and one who appears to take everything seriously. He's also had to work for his stardom.

In the ego-revolving world of Hollywood this onetime oil-field worker and Harvard graduate via a scholarship – Damon at this point still had to complete two semesters to achieve – who talks in an accent as thick as a Dallas traffic jam is a true leading man but without the usual posturing. Tommy Lee Jones is a grown-up star and on *The Good Old Boys* became something of a father figure to Damon, who read all he could about Jones' career.

He learned that Jones is the original combustible cowboy who has made more than forty movies and appeared in landmark television productions like *The Executioner's Song* – as the 'I want to die' killer, Gary Gilmore – and most memorably in 1989's Western *Lonesome Dove*. From a cast of hundreds, including Robert Duvall and Anjelica Huston, he stole the show by saying very little indeed. Much as he did in *Batman Forever*, for in that Hollywood happenstance he was the senior bad boy Harvey Two-Face for Chris O'Donnell's Boy Wonder debut.

For *The Good Old Boys* Jones acted as star, director and screenplay writer. Matt Damon played his son, a young Texan who leaves the Lone Star state and his family, dreaming of building motor cars. Damon learned things but sometimes the long, Texan way around. Jones told him about stardom – it's like being thrown from a horse. If you can't ride him without spurs don't get back

on. He also taught him about grace in the spotlight.

After scoring, to most people's pleasure, the Best Supporting Oscar for his obsessed Marshal Gerard in *The Fugitive*, he gave another great performance accepting his statuette saying: 'The only thing a man can say at a time like this ... I am not really bald.' He reported not to the champagne reception but to bed and work the next morning at 6 a.m.

'Everybody wanted to work with Tommy Lee Jones', said Damon, going on: 'Getting the chance was terrific for me. Even after all he has done he is cautious and it is a great lesson. He said that on every movie he's called home and said: "I'm making the best movie I've ever made - possibly the best movie that's ever been made in the history of the media." And adds: "Then it turns out to be a howling pooch." There's no bullshit about movies with him and I like that for there's so much of it about. He's also very funny – I learned that was a defensive thing with him. It's something I think I've always used but probably not always been aware of.

'And there is that wonderful sense of self – a treasure if you have it. He tells one story – and there's a movie in it. It's about his childhood. I don't know how true it is but he says: "I've talked myself into believing I remember the day that I was born. I hang on to my memories with cat's claws. I can remember tornadoes in Knox County when I was three. We were living in a trailer next to the hospital and near a cotton field. The tornado jumped over our trailer and hit the hospital. I remember seeing X-rays from the hospital floating down over the cotton plants in bloom. Some of my memories are clear – very clear. Both my mother and my father used to go to honky-tonk bars to do what everybody in that part of Texas did – drink. I'd wait for them outside in the car, alone. I remember hearing music and singing coming through the walls of the saloon to me in the car. I remember lying there just waiting, just waiting alone."

'That's wonderful stuff. What do you learn from a man like that? I think you learn things you won't know about until years from now.'

For Matt Damon, the lessons from home, college, his friends and family and the movie stars he worked closely with, like Jones on location in Alpine, Texas, fuelled his belief in himself, his determination to be noticed.

He admits now that he may have pursued his dreams too vigorously. He could have killed himself.

At a glance his role in *Courage Under Fire* was not one that an actor would could to the limit for but instinctively Damon realized it was his chance at being taken seriously by the big-timers, the movers and shakers, the people who made and got movies made. He was thinking of Benicio Del Toro and *The Usual Suspects* when he decided how to handle this chance.

The film was a powerful drama set in the aftermath of the Gulf War, requiring strong performances from co-stars Meg Ryan and Denzel Washington. Matt Damon's first problem with the film was his mother. She later explained: 'I was deeply against the Gulf War and I didn't know how the film was going to pan politically. It was hard for me to visit Matt on the set of *Courage Under Fire*.' There were to be other family concerns but about Damon – not the movie.

⭐ **On the trail Way Out West.**

Geronimo!

← Previous spread
✪ **Leading the posse, *Rawhide*-style, with hero Robert Duvall.**

It was a star vehicle and something different for Meg Ryan. The plot involved an investigation by Denzel Washington into whether Ryan's character, Captain Karen Walden, who died during the desert conflict, was entitled to the US Medal of Honour.

One witness to her deeds is Damon's Sergeant Ilario. He must tell about her conduct in battle but is haunted by his own. Back in America he has become hooked on heroin. To get the addict look the young star lost forty pounds in weight – a little less than three stone – from his already athletic body. He did this in just three months. 'He was obsessive about it,' said his brother Kyle, adding: 'We were all worried about him.'

But Matt Damon's only concern was to make a lasting impression: 'I was convinced I need to lose up to forty-five pounds for the role. Because I was an unknown the studio wouldn't pay for a nutritionist so I did it on my own by eating a lot of protein and running thirteen miles a day for three months solid. There's a very short list of young actors in Los Angeles and I thought this movie could help me to climb a little higher in the pecking order. I felt he should be a shell of a man by the end of the story – not just because of the drugs he's been taking but because of the guilt he feels eating away at him.

'It was the hardest thing I've ever had to do. I ran six miles in the morning and seven miles at night and I'd drink four to six pots of coffee to be able to run that distance. When I went into a restaurant the first thing I would tell waiters was: "I'm your worst nightmare".'

'I wouldn't waiver from my diet. It got so bad that when my girlfriend kissed me I'd have to wash my mouth out because I could taste the oils on her lips from the food she'd eaten.

'I remember seeing Lou Diamond Phillips who has boxing scenes in the film and looks magnificent and thinking: "God, if I looked like that I wouldn't take my shirt off." I thought he looked fat.'

He admits to clearly becoming anorexic: 'It was a business decision. I thought: "Nobody will take this role because it's too small. If I go out of my way to make something of this ... I was sick of reading scripts that Chris O'Donnell had passed on and I was looking for something to set me apart. "Look what I'll do, I'll kill myself!" '

Director Edward Zwick, who was used to working with dedicated young actors – he guided Brad Pitt in *Legends of the Fall* – had agreed with Damon's 'reading' of the role and the need for him

to lose weight. When Damon reported for work on location in Texas the director freaked. Damon said: 'He was scared and told me to start eating but at that point I was so far gone I wasn't going to compromise.'

'I'm not sorry I did it. I knew it was a great role with a real chance to do something I hadn't done before. I so wanted to be recognized for my role I was willing to kill myself for it. I really damaged my body and the effects lasted for two years. I just didn't know the effects would be so long lasting. When you treat your body like that you wear it out and it's so unhealthy. I was under two per cent body fat. I went to a doctor in Massachusetts General in Boston after I got back from shooting

the picture and he said: "The good news is your heart didn't shrink." But my blood sugar was all messed up. I did a bunch of stuff to my body but it's coming back into kilter and it's kind of everything in moderation now. I'm bouncing back and I should be one hundred per cent again.'

Medically, he had an anorexia-like condition from doing the opposite of what his hero Robert De Niro did for *Raging Bull*, gaining more than forty pounds to play boxer Jake LaMotta. 'I was amazed to watch his discipline,' said Lou Diamond Phillips. 'He kept to a diet of steamed chicken breast and steamed vegetables and that was it. Matt likes to eat so this was a huge undertaking for him.'

Working on *Courage Under Fire* he was thin – and starstruck. He says he started quoting lines from Denzel Washington's title role in *Malcolm X* and laughs: 'I think I knew more of it than he did. He was so amazed but I was such a fan. And with Meg Ryan – the same. She's a real role model of dealing with the business. I asked Meg how she can have a family and work in this business, how she can deal with it all. I was lucky to work with her and good human beings who really do care about family and things that are to me also more important. The movie was a learning experience because I got more perspectives from people I respect. From Meg I learned so much about being a person as well as being a star. And being in control.'

As his own love life was falling apart – 'losing the love of my life' – he was intrigued by Ryan's apparent ability to have it all. In turn she was taken by Damon's dedication – it reminded her of her husband Dennis Quaid – for what amounted to only two days of filming. It was grand-theft scene-stealing. Something Ryan is also good at.

She and Damon have talked about projects together but with their dual commitments it will not happen until at the earliest 2000. Meg Ryan's always been more Gap than Gucci, the heroine of fluster films about befuddled love – those with a beginning, muddle and hopeful ending – and consequently her image is of an old-style Hollywood dizzy dame.

Her severe, square, black reading glasses do nothing to deflate that bubbly blonde image. Rather, they add to it. She's even cuter. Almost as alluring to someone like Matt Damon is her movie balance sheet. She was aged thirty-six in 1998 and had made twenty-two films and her comedies have made magical box office arithmetic of more than $850 million dollars in America alone. She surprised Damon, telling him she was changing the rules.

Previously she was content to simply sell her services to the movies but she's now a working mother and having triumphed domestically – much to her surprise – she wants more control of her professional life. Her new, more mature attitude is visible at breakfast time in the penthouse suite of a Beverly Hills hotel. Previously with Meg Ryan it was casual wear, coffee, cookies, giggles and throaty laughs. She was always serious about her work and her life but a remarkable metamorphosis is clear. Ironically, given her reservation: 'When I wear high heels I have a great vocabulary and I speak in paragraphs. I'm more eloquent. I plan to wear them more often.'

There's a hint less confidence when she admits: 'It's scary to change a formula which has worked but it was time at work – and at home.' She says her new look reflects not just a spicier view of life but her need to be in control. Privately, she has always been tough and helped actor Dennis Quaid conquer cocaine addiction before she agreed to marry him in 1990. Ryan, who made her screen debut at age fifteen, a funky adolescent

'I'm not sorry I did it. I knew it was a great role with a real chance to do something I hadn't done before. **I so wanted to be recognized for my role I was willing to kill myself for it.'**

with a wistful, faraway, safe smile, has grown up. But not, as many thought, to become just another Doris Day, a fluff in a lithe, dancer's body, the perennial girl-next-door star.

Nora Ephron, who wrote Ryan's breakthrough film *When Harry Met Sally ...* (1989) and directed her landmark movie *Sleepless in Seattle* (1993) believes she knows what has made Ryan a major power-player: she is liked by both men and women, on and off screen. And Damon is the male equivalent. Ephron observes: 'She has no vanity. The women that women love are women who don't walk around full of their own self-love. You absolutely know when you see Meg on screen that if you found yourself next to her you might become friends.'

Damon might do well to listen to her lessons in Hollywood dealings: 'I've been in this business for years and I'm still befuddled by the ways of this town. Sometimes a studio will send me a script and say would I like to produce with them. Or would I like to be "attached" to the project. Or can they "sneak" me a script. I know that as soon as I put down the phone they'll be trying to "sneak" it to someone else. I like to understand the logical progression of things but this business is just too convoluted.'

As Matt Damon discovered when he became a 'golden boy'. He was astonished: 'The funny thing is that as soon as you get big the studios send you

these scripts that they've been trying to get made for twenty years, that were originally written for Dustin Hoffman. They've been sitting on the shelf. You get their old stand-bys.' Stand-bys with, of course, multi-million dollar offers. Meg Ryan says of Damon : 'He still has much to learn but he has a lot of depth to work from.'

Love and Hollywood are certainly forces Matt Damon is still learning about but he's never had problems getting the ladies. Keeping them has been more difficult. His Ripley director spotted the Lothario factor immediately. Anthony Minghella says: 'There's something so apple pie about him. You know he was the best-looking kid in his school, won all the awards at track and field and dated the most popular girl.'

Casey Affleck says of his brother's best friend: 'The thing about Matt and girls is that he's totally fair – he likes them all. They can be blonde or brunettes and he'll be smitten. He's a legs man though. He likes long legs. And the girls certainly seem to like him. Oh, yeah, they like his smile but he's a lucky guy for he seems to appeal to all of them. The girls wanted him to take them home.'

Matt Damon was the one who took Skylar Satenstein home – and to meet the family. But unfortunately he couldn't hold her. She left him for a heavy metal rock star.

Chapter 4

Lover Boy

'It was a long-distance romance.'
Matt Damon on trying to
explain losing the 'love of my life'

With his fame flourishing Matt Damon had won a reputation as one of Hollywood's leading ladykillers. Everyone he encountered appeared to fall for his charm – some much more than others. But all along he nursed a romantic and – depending on his mood – sometimes bitter secret.

With much persuasion, Matt Damon can be coaxed into admitting he still carries a torch for Skylar Satenstein. She was a medical student at Columbia University while he was studying at Harvard and moonlighting as an actor. A New Yorker, Skylar is tall and gorgeous with sun-streaked hair and Damon makes another confession: 'She was the love of my life.'

They were closely involved in their early college years but Hollywood became what he calls 'the other woman'. Damon was working on and around movies and could see less and less of Skylar. They talked on the phone, exchanged thousands of words on e-mail, but it got difficult.

'We were college sweethearts. I was in Los Angeles. She was at Columbia – it was a long-distance romance which was really hard. We did it for years and then it looked like the dynamic was becoming so fucked up because we were trying to avoid the thing of not seeing each other for a long time and then being extra careful not to say something that might upset the other one. We decided to leave it to the gods – if it's meant to be, it's meant to be.

'And then she married someone else.'

He takes time after that – it still hurts. To an inquiry if the new husband was also a doctor, he revealed his feelings: 'No, he's a fucking rock star who's got $80 million and his own jet.'

The details of drummer Lars Ulrich's bank account are not confirmed by the rocker from the heavy metal band Metallica but he does have a private jet. He and Skylar dated for nearly a year before marrying in Las Vegas in February, 1997. It remains an ongoing bad memory for Damon but luckily he was able to concentrate on what had ended the affair – his Hollywood career.

The romantic crash with Skylar was at the same time Matt Damon started work on his first showcase role. He was indeed *The Rainmaker* for he had already formed the clouds which would soon pour success by co-writing *Good Will Hunting*, which was to be filmed later that year. He was ready for work and, as it turned out, romance.

First, he had to meet the man often thought of as the Godfather of Hollywood. The reviews for his 'shattering' performance in *Courage Under Fire* had been tremendous, with America's *People* magazine calling attention to Damon's role, showing the decimation, physical and emotional, of war. Certainly, after all the arguably foolhardy effort, he got the result he wanted. He was noticed.

✪ **The Big Squeeze for Minnie Driver, between Matt and Ben Affleck.**

⭐ 'Yes, Godfather.' Matt takes advice from director Francis Ford Coppola.

And not just by the critics. Francis Ford Coppola was interested in him taking the leading role – one which has him on screen for virtually all of its 137 minutes – in an adaptation of John Grisham's *The Rainmaker*. Grisham, who is cemented in the worldwide bestseller lists, is always careful about who gets the lead roles in the movies from his books. Coppola has always been a stickler over casting. And all of Damon's peers from the Frat Pack, back and forward, wanted the role of the young lawyer Rudy Baylor.

'We chose Matt out of about six or seven good choices,' says Coppola through that familiar big beard and the legendary director added: 'Ed Norton was one of the choices, from the young, promising kids. After all is said and done I wanted the movie to have a good heart. I felt that had to come from this kid and what his inner life was.

'Matt provided that. As an individual he's a

Lover Boy

The table is always laid in old-fashioned Italian style and recipes which haven't been followed in the Old Country for more than fifty years are in use. For it's that history which still spices the life of Francis Coppola and his family: the Genco olive oil, the peppers, tomatoes, pasta (lots of the child-hood macaroni), oranges, pungent basil leaves, mozzarella, champagne vinegar with cranberries, sun-dried tomatoes in olive oil, merlot vinaigrette and, of course, that staple of Italian pastry, the cannolis. In *The Godfather*, when Michael Corleone is being instructed on the finer points of the restaurant execution of a New York police captain, the *capo* Clemenza emphasizes: 'Leave the gun, take the cannolis.'

The first two *Godfather* films (they earned more than $700 million at the box office and another $200 million on video, as well as twenty-one Academy Award nominations and nine actual Oscars), the award-winning *The Conversation* (with Damon favourite Gene Hackman) and the seminal *Apocalypse Now*, have made him fabulously famous and wealthy. When he cast Damon in *The Rainmaker* the young actor says he thought he was dreaming: 'I thought I'd wake up and find I was just an understudy – that another actor, Steve Dorff (another contender) or somebody really had the role.'

The film-maker who once flew from California to London 'for lunch' is one of Hollywood's most magnificent obsessions. A big bear of a man with a pasta stomach and a salt-and-pepper beard – often dusted with Parmesan – he created his own film studio, Zoetrope, in 1980. But it could not survive a commercial flop: *One from the Heart* did a belly flop at the box office. The splash put Coppola at the centre of a financial labyrinth that tower blocks of lawyers found themselves attempting to sort out.

Coppola's answer to money problems – and it has always been the same one – is to work. He had the rights to two of S. H. Hinton's books aimed at young adults: *The Outsiders* and *Rumble Fish*.

Rumble Fish is about a tragic triangle formed by

fabulous kid; very bright. He's a great person to work with, willing to go through any stuff that you put him through. He has his own head, comes up with ideas and dialogue but he's also a team player who works great with the other actors.'

Coppola has proved how wonderful he is with young actors, boosting the fledgling careers of Al Pacino, James Caan, Harrison Ford, Matt Dillon and his own Oscar-winning nephew Nicolas Cage. It is, he says, a family sort of thing. Matt Damon found that when he went to dinner at the Casa Coppola.

Matt Damon   45

a father played by Dennis Hopper and his two sons, the cool motorcycle-riding Mickey Rourke and the wannabe-cool Matt Dillon. Father and sons, men and boys, young versus old: constant Coppola themes. The film launched Rourke's career, which would proceed through many twists and turns, ups and downs.

He was back in the mainstream in *The Rainmaker* as Bruiser Stone, the unorthodox legal entrepreneur who takes on Damon's young Rudy on what can politely be described as a contingency basis. Rourke closely watched the Coppola–Damon relationship and it brought back glowing memories for him: 'Matt worked his ass off. Matt walked the walk. And Francis showed a lot of love on the set. Francis is good with young kids.'

That showed so much on *The Rainmaker*, as did his love of strong actors like Rourke, Jon Voight and Danny DeVito. The simple story has Damon going up against smoothie big-time lawyer Voight

Tennessee, the local newspapers quizzed him about how he would handle his accent. He had thought of that, having found a job as a barman in Knoxville, Tennessee, and exposed himself to every conceivable 'southern drawl' – drunk and sober – he thought possible. At the end he managed a hybrid Knoxville/Memphis/Nashville accent he kept working on during long film days. Mary Kay Place, who starred as Rudy's client's mother, was moved by him: 'He has a huge heart. He really worked at the film, worked more than anybody to make it a success.'

At first, Damon admits that it was a good show. He not only was playing the young, in-experienced Rudy Baylor – he felt like him making the movie. A more relaxed Damon sat in the gardens of Coppola's estate and talked about the movie: 'I felt outgunned a lot of the time but Francis was very good at putting me at ease. A lot of the acting games he plays and the way he

'I fell in love with her', says Damon, gushing, 'Who wouldn't? She's fabulous.'

in a wrongful death insurance case. Subplots involve Claire Danes – only eighteen in 1997 – as an abused wife whom Rudy helps and falls for. Life would imitate art.

All the impressive names around him, cult veterans like Dean Stockwell and Roy Scheider, shook Damon's confidence. 'Those guys are legends – and role models.' But in turn they all told him he was Rudy. Even John Grisham assured him he had become the character. He had worked at it. From Meg Ryan he had learned how to turn around preconceived notions of a character by use of voice and movement; from Robert Duvall the need to 'become' the character you were playing, to make them 'real'.

Before filming began proper in Memphis,

treats you is very paternal and we rehearsed up here and he made me live in his house. He became my godfather. I am his godson now. He had me live in his son Roman's bedroom and in the morning he would make me breakfast before we'd go to rehearse. I was totally daunted when I showed up.

'I had this bag on my shoulder and I was horrified. I had just been eating at MacDonald's the day before and suddenly I was up at Francis' house but he relaxed me, my fear was assuaged pretty quickly.

'It was the same with John Grisham. This was the sixth film that had been made from one of his books and he really wanted to put me at my ease and took me aside and told me I was going to be

⭐ **A face to fall in love with: Claire Danes.**

great. He said I had the accent down, he was very, very complimentary and very positive. It was good. Had they been stand-offish – Francis and Grisham, had they been austere and stand-offish, I probably would have been horrified but they were both really compassionate, good guys.

'Francis is an effing genius, pure and simple. Working with him was wonderful. Everyone had a ball. There was just one embarrassing story which involved *The Godfather*. I know every line of the

movie. Me and my friends used to sit around, drink beers and watch the movie dozens of times. So anyway, I went to San Francisco to do some post-production work on *The Rainmaker* and one night there was a première for the re-release of *The Godfather*. I went with Danny DeVito and sat with him and Sherry Lansing. I had never seen it on the big screen because I was only two when the movie came out.

'Before the movie started I said to Sherry: "This is cool, I've never seen it on the big screen. She looks at the guy next to her and says: "See, Al, Matt's never seen it either."

'Then Al Pacino peeks around Sherry and says: "You've never seen it on the big screen? Me neither. I saw it on TV but never on the big screen." I was so stunned to be looking at Al Pacino I just said: "Well, it's good and you did a good job." Then I kinda leaned back in my char and felt like such a putz.'

But Pacino and Sherry Lansing, the Paramount Studio executive and the first woman to head a Hollywood studio (20th Century Fox) just went back to watching the movie – on the big screen. The film will always be the real treasure of Coppola's celluloid legacy but Damon feels he has seen another and even longer-lasting aspect of the moviemaker:

'Francis is intriguing because he wants to harness all that energy that is out there in people like me. He's got this whole computer programme he's setting up where he's going to take anybody who wants, any young person who wants to be in the movie business, and they can read from any book, play or movie on a one-minute cassette and send it with a head shot (photograph) and he's going to bank them in his computer so he can call up any image or voice – he can literally start thinking of casting people off his computer.

'He's very tuned to the fact that there is a lot of energy out there and he's one person who is offering a chance, something positive.

'Hey, I got to make *The Rainmaker* because of these sort of methods, of calling in people. I knew the film was being made and Francis was involved but that was all I knew. I couldn't find out anything else so I read the book just in case something came up quickly which is just what happened. I got this phone call at 5 p.m. and they said: "You have a screen test in Memphis tomorrow." I was on the plane! They faxed me the script and when I got to the hotel I read the scenes. I never even unpacked. I absolutely thought I wasn't going to get the job. I mean, what were the chances? Slim to none,

⭐ **Walking Tall: with** *Rainmaker* **co-star Danny DeVito.**

right? But it was New Year's Eve and I was getting a chance to audition for Coppola. Am I a moron? No. I took the chance …

'All the lawyer stuff was new to me – I always wanted to be an actor from when I was very young, from about twelve. I knew that was what I wanted to do but I always wanted to play a lawyer. I saw George C. Scott do Darrow and I had front-row seats. I remember getting hit with the spit and everything and thinking: "Wow, if some-day when I'm sixty years old and I can be that powerful I will really have lived." The command that he had of me and everybody else in the the-atre was awesome and I remember wishing that I could do that. And Francis gave me the chance to play a lawyer. But I think that was just because of Claire … '

Claire Danes in 1998 was becoming the most sought-after actress in the world. But Hollywood had to take a back seat in September, 1998, when aged nineteen she began her freshman year at Yale University – something Jodie Foster, who had directed her in *Home for the Holidays*, had done eighteen years earlier. To Danes the achievements of Foster – Oscars for *Silence of he Lambs* and *The Accused* and applause for directing films like *Little Man Tate* – convinced her that Tinseltown ambition and university could mix. Where Matt Damon had found it tricky balancing Harvard and Hollywood she felt she could do both. But as Foster points out, Claire Danes has had one of the most glamorous adolescences ever. She says: 'When I was five I decided I was going to be an actress. When I was first finding out that people went to college somebody said: "Yale has a great drama school" and I said: "OK, well I'm going to Yale." '

Her confidence is astonishing – and she has seen the full impact of celebrity fame having co-starred with Leonardo DiCaprio in *Romeo and Juliet*. She remains amazed at what has happened to him: 'We were at the *Man in the Iron Mask* première together and he got up to walk across to see his mother and the entire side of the room

stood up and followed him. There were sixty people and they just followed him. It's beyond weird. But he's so charismatic. There are some people who are just really engaging.'

Like Matt Damon. And Danes herself. 'I fell in love with her,' says Damon, gushing, 'Who wouldn't? She's fabulous.'

She was also hip and cool having completed the movie version of Aaron Spelling's ground-breaking television series *The Mod Squad*. She took the role originated by Peggy Lipton who became an early Seventies icon through the series. The big-screen version only validated more Danes' super-status. She was already an Internet pin-up from her time in a youth television series; had rejected a part in Steven Spielberg's *Schindler's List*; snared a never-screened pilot for a Dudley Moore TV sit-com; made *The Rainmaker* for Coppola and *U-Turn* for Oliver Stone; filmed *Les Miserables* for Bille August in Prague in 1997; and the following year made *Polish Wedding* with Gabriel Byrne. She was so understandably busy she had to turn down the title role in a big-budget *Joan of Arc* being filmed in

late 1998 by Luc Besson and starring his wife Milla Jacovich. She also appeared in *To Gillian On Her 37th Birthday* opposite Michelle Pfeiffer. Then, of course, *Romeo and Juliet*.

She was seeing her Beverly Hills psychiatrist twice a week when she met Matt Damon on the set of *The Rainmaker*. For him it was an inside look at what Hollywood can and cannot do and what you have to do to cope with the success and the rejection. For Claire Danes it was all attention after director Baz Luhrmann's wild-in-the-streets version of the Shakespeare romance. The Australian director said: 'I saw many young actresses from around the world. I had to have someone who looked fifteen but was in control of her craft. When I had them it was a moment-by-moment collaboration. Those moments of rehearsals were very sweet moments. We had fun trying to understand the text. One of the things we set out to do was to get them to claim the language for

Matt is quick to add, **'But not all of my girlfriends have been actresses'.** But the woman who followed Claire Danes certainly was …

themselves, to make the words their own.'

Claire Danes coped with that. And the kidnapping of a film-crew member on location in Mexico City. Her mother was also taken to hospital with pneumonia. That also resolved itself. But she says she was terrified when it came to filming the immortal balcony scene: 'That was so intimidating to do. I mean, it was ridiculous to get so worked up about it but I did. I had to go on and say those famous lines that have been made fun of over the years. I had to throw all these other performances and interpretations behind me and start from scratch.

'I had such a panic attack. I'd just seen the Olivia Hussey version [Franco Zeffirelli's 1968 film] and she was so gorgeous. So I had a little break-down at three in the morning. I'm self-conscious about my looks; I'm not secure in that area. It's, like, amazing how frightening that is.' Luhrmann, like Coppola would later, supported her: 'The filming was a lot more extreme than anyone imagined or bargained for. The reason I chose Claire is I knew she could sustain the work and its intensity. Claire is an incredibly hard worker and methodical. You simply forget she's her age.'

The actress herself believes she's just been in rehearsals for most of her life: 'It's like I'm becoming more of a woman and more of an established actress at the same time. It's like all this practising as a teenager is finally paying off.'

For Claire Danes it is not a question about who she wants to be but how fast she wants to be it. 'She is one of the most exciting actresses to debut in the past ten years,' says Steven Spielberg who

has become one of the most renowned and respected arbiters of young Hollywood talent. Danes appears a one-of-a-kind, saying: 'I live in an adult world but I'm a kid. There are a lot of opinions coming at me. It's insane. People my age really need to have downtime, to chill, to be really pretentious and talk about pseudo-intellectual ideas. I haven't gotten too much of that which I'm really missing.'

Her psychiatrist? 'The doctor gives me permission to accept that I am human, which I need … '

Matt Damon saw a perfect human. Their romance was an old-style movie romance, the emotions displayed on screen spilled into their off-screen lives. It began before the movie did: 'Claire and I screen-tested together and I think Francis wanted Claire so badly that I kind of got lumped in because I was the one who was lucky enough to read with her. We did the scenes in the hospital cafeteria and then the scene where I take her to her room in the wheelchair. I felt I could do more with it. I felt what I did wasn't enough.

'I always really feel I want to keep going but obviously it was enough. Claire really helped. She's an amazing person and an amazing actress. Francis likened her to a violinist, a prodigy. I was baffled watching her work because she's so young and yet emotionally honest. People train their whole lives to do that and still don't get it right. She's a wonderful person and we were close. I learned a lot from her.'

Matt is quick to add, 'But not all of my girlfriends have been actresses.' But the woman who followed Claire Danes certainly was ….

Chapter 5

Medusa

'Minnie Driver's audition for Good Will Hunting *was one of the handful of really great, memorable auditions I've ever seen.'*

the movies producer, Lawrence Bender

The critics enthusiastically applauded *The Rainmaker*, most singling out Matt Damon. Prominent television and print reviewer Gene Siskel spoke for most of them when he told a nationwide US television audience: 'The discovery here is a fresh young talent, actor Matt Damon. It's the acting that is so good.' The movie's box office and critical success was perfectly timed, exciting encouragement for Damon and Affleck's hopes for *Good Will Hunting* which was to be released only a few weeks later. It had seemed it would never happen.

By the beginning of 1997 they had been at work on their movie for five years, writing it on cross-country trips, by phone and fax to each other from faraway locations, on tables in other's people's apartments and in long improvisation sessions – Damon talking into a tape-recorder, Affleck typing. At the end Damon admits: 'A lot of it came from our own inexperience as writers, just not knowing where to take the story. We had well over one thousand pages of these characters and we didn't know what to do with them.'

'We thought,' said Ben Affleck, 'that we needed to insert an element that would sell the script but we were lucky enough to run into people who were smart enough to say: "You don't

need that." We were reluctant at first because we thought that was what everyone was supposed to want. We figured it needed an antagonist but the movie doesn't really have an antagonist which is more interesting to us because it's more ambiguous but we didn't know you were allowed to make a movie without a bad guy.'

His partner said: 'We were told: "Make this story very small and it's OK." That was a tremendous burden lifted from our shoulders. We stuck to writing about things and people we knew. It was written in fits and starts – we get inspired and then boom-boom-boom, a lot of stuff comes out and then you sit around not knowing what to do next.

'It was a combination of things, not the least of which were speeches which had been thrown our way by our own parents – and even if we didn't understand those things we understand them enough to repeat them!!

'This was a different sort of film. Ben's done *Armageddon* with Bruce Willis which is a giant action film and when you're doing the action shots often there's very little movie being made per hour as posed to when you are doing dialogue-heavy scenes.

✪ **A bewitching look – the face that launched a tempestuous romance.**

✪ Minnie Driver confronts Chris O'Donnell.

It's a different talent to amp yourself up for moments of running when you're supposed to be conveying fear for only five seconds of film. On *Courage Under Fire* I only did two days with Denzel Washington and a month of running around in the desert for the same amount of screen time. There were days when I thought: "Oh, God, when is this ever going to end?" It would take so long just to set up the shots.'

Good Will Hunting was by contrast a family affair. Even the stars' mothers are glimpsed in the background in a restaurant scene. The film contrasts Boston's academic community with the tough neighbourhood side and caught in between is Will Hunting. As written by Damon and Affleck, he is an amazing character, a rough diamond of a genius with a great body, an ability to solve the most complex maths problems and a photographic memory. But the script, acting and Gus Van Sant's handling saved the movie from being forgettable fantasy-factory fodder.

✪ **Good will pitching – Matt in award-winning character and action.**

✪ **Minnie Driver confronts Chris O'Donnell.**

There were some critical ponderings over the believability of Damon's mathematical genius. But at Britain's Warwick University Professor Ian Stewart whose book *Does God Play Dice?* became a bestseller, said: 'There are people like Matt Damon's character. We had one at Warwick. He never went to lectures. He'd borrow someone else's notes the day before an exam and get ninety-five per cent – ninety on a bad day. The question that he and the film raised was, if you have that kind of gift, do you want it? We tried to persuade him to do a Ph.D but he wanted to get out, get a job. I've no idea what happened to him.'

Most of us know what happened to Matt Damon. But the outcome – like that of *Good Will Hunting* – was never certain. As in most of his previous films, Van Sant focuses revealingly on the attitudes of and to an outsider, of society's misfits, and the juggling of the brain and the heart. The director said: 'Matt has a great face so that's always great. But what makes him appealing is he's

⭐ **Fancy a cigarette? The lull before the storm both on and off screen with Minnie Driver.**

bringing a character to life so specifically that it's mesmerising.'

But the film still works because of the script, which has Will Hunting avoiding jail by agreeing to be supervised by a psychotherapist, a role which gave Robin Williams an Oscar on his fourth nomination. 'There's a great intelligence in Matt and Ben and a great playfulness,' says Williams with some glee as he sits talking in a Beverly Hills hotel. 'I'm still surprised by the fact that those two boys – and that's what they are – wrote this story that has, I think, a great depth to it. All the characters are well drawn out and the relationships are complex.'

When the cameras finally rolled, so did the tears. Matt Damon and Ben Affleck were weeping when filming began on *Good Will Hunting* in April 1997. 'There was this meaningful moment,' says co-producer Chris Moore. 'The cast and crew started applauding and the pair of them realized: "We are making this movie – that is Robin Williams over there saying our lines." '

Robin Williams says he was taken by the scene: 'They had the dream a long time ago and it finally was happening. It was wonderful to watch.' Damon later recalled: 'When Ben and I sold *Good Will Hunting* we almost died. Then when Gus Van Sant agreed to do it we died again. I mean, the guy is an effing genius. Then it was unbelievable when Robin Williams agreed to be in it.'

Much of what happened is the responsibility of Lawrence Bender who produced the film. Following on from success with Quentin Tarantino and movies like *Reservoir Dogs*, *Pulp Fiction* and

'We all knew what just happened was extraordinary and we didn't want to break the moment. We all said: "We've got our gal."' **Matt Damon said it loudest.**

Jackie Brown. Bender says his star-making – and resurrecting, most notably with John Travolta in *Pulp Fiction* – has evolved into something of a philosophy: 'Quentin and I – maybe because we come from acting – we treat actors like stars and stars like actors. I mean, I can't take credit for making Matt Damon a star but I was very involved in *Good Will Hunting*. I had a lot to do with that in terms of casting, of shaping the script. Matt came out of that a fucking star.

'What's great about him is he's a star who can act. And he's a very grounded guy. Both he and Ben Affleck are incredibly talented and serve the hype unlike a lot of other people. George Clooney in *From Dawn Till Dusk* where Robert Rodriguez shot him like he was shooting a woman made him look macho and beautiful and though he was a star on TV, on *E.R.*, he hadn't really crossed over yet and this made him into a superstar.

'There are things you can't plan for. Like *Good Will Hunting*. After the film critics' awards in New York we were all snowed up in a blizzard and there was this fun group in the bar of the Four Seasons Hotel. Harvey Weinstein leaned over to me very excited, drinking champagne and said: "Lawrence I've got my next great script, it's my favourite movie at Miramax and you're the first person I'm asking to come on it." I read the script and it moved me so much I cried. It wasn't even one of those polished, professional scripts that "looks" right. This one was fresh, new. It reminded me a little of reading *Reservoir Dogs*. It wasn't even always typed correctly but it had an innocence, a rawness that made it all the more endearing.

'It's not about the package, it's about the content. When I got it I worked with Matt and Ben on strengthening the characters and working on the "architecture". I learned a lot. Sometimes I was right, sometimes wrong. Out of this collaboration was a really beautiful movie. Everyone on it had these amazing talents that were able to come out. Nobody had entourages, nobody had ego. For me, all the stars lined up.

'When an actor comes into a room to audition for me or Quentin we're looking for very real, naturalistic performances, because the performances need to be extremely personal and real.

'Minnie Driver's audition for *Good Will Hunting* was one of the handful of really great, memorable auditions I've ever seen. There were five guys in the room: me, Chris Moore, Matt Damon, Ben Affleck and Gus Van Sant. Minnie came in and started reading with Matt and he was like: "OK, I'm just going to start reading with another person." It was a really good script and it was with Gus Van Sant so lots of people wanted to come in. Matt wasn't ready for somebody who was going to be so good. It was like you could see him going: "I better be good too!" They read the scene where he tells her he doesn't love her and when they finished the scene there was absolute silence.

'It was like when you're in a movie theatre and you're crying but you don't want to look at the person next to you, so you go into your own intimate world. All five of us had a little tear in our eye and were embarrassed to look at each other. We all knew what just happened was extraordinary and we didn't want to break the moment. We all said: "We've got our gal." '

Matt Damon said it loudest .

Chapter 6

Oscar and Minnie

'I just said to Matt: "Losing would suck and winning would be really scary." And it is really, really scary...'

Ben Affleck, post-Oscars, 1998

Minnie Driver is tall with a toned, bountiful figure and thick, black Medusa-style hair framing startling eyes and cheekbones. She is striking. And so is her attitude. Her romance with Matt Damon was one of the most talked about in Hollywood – by other people.

He ended their relationship in front of millions of people on live television. It was on Oprah Winfrey's show that Damon mumbled about their high-profile, 'golden couple' relationship: 'I care about her a lot.' The 'but' hung in the air and he added: 'We kind of decided it wasn't meant to be.'

There was a difficulty about that. Minnie Driver – the same age as Damon, whom she had been sleeping with for seven months; one of Britain's most prominent and sought-after exports to Hollywood; his co-star in *Good Will Hunting* and hundreds of worldwide gossip columns; an Oscar nominee as Best Supporting Actress for her role in that movie as Skylar, the lover named after Damon's lost love – thought the romance was still going strong.

Damon, on 12 January 1998, rather shattered that belief.

Of course, it made their romance even more exciting gossip, now there was a focus. It was only

months later that Minnie Driver was willing to talk about it all and in July of what should have been a brilliant year – Hollywood success, Oscar acclaim – she revealed: 'It stings now and again. It makes for better copy where there's a victim but I have to say it's the worst casting of my entire career.'

Indeed, when the romance began she was most certainly the emotionally stronger of the two and her poise was provocatively obvious when she appeared at the Academy Awards in a head-turning red Halston dress. She is used to people looking at her. Like Lawrence Bender, Matt Damon has her audition etched in his mind: 'It must have been real daunting because there were five guys staring at her. She was quite extraordinary, to the point where I had to stop her in the middle of her reading because I got tongue-tied just looking at her.'

Later, he admitted that it might have been better had he been similarly tongue-tied on Oprah. Romance with leading ladies seems an occupational hazard for him – he was close-up with Bridget Hall when they were making *School*

⭐ **The Boys with the Oscars: Matt, Robin Williams and Ben Affleck with their 1998 Academy Awards.**

'I've got a better seat than Jack Nicholson', laughed Damon about his idol and fellow nominee.

Ties in 1992 – but he said that, with the woman who brought his screen Skylar to life: 'There's no risk. Minnie is so professional. When somebody is a good actress they can get through a scene no matter what.'

Gus Van Sant had the eye-finder view of their romance – how they fell in love. Their big scene in *Good Will Hunting*, the one used at rehearsal, is after they make love and then Will tells Skylar he does not love her. Van Sant did a number of takes to get it just right. 'He was resetting the clock,' according to Minnie Driver who added: 'You adjust to fit the person you're working with and that's why, perhaps, you fall in love with them.'

Van Sant saw something early on in filming but said: 'It was difficult to tell if there was a game being played or true romance.' There was an element of game – Minnie Driver had another man in her life but she defends herself: 'I was just blinded by the light of somebody else. With film romances you'll tell yourself: "This was valid. It was part of this place in my life but maybe it's not appropriate to bring it home." '

Home by then was Los Angeles where Driver now has her own film production company, Two Drivers, with her sister. The thirty-year-old Kate remembers: 'From the minute she could open her mouth, Min was going to be an actress. In Barbados where we grew up, we used to act around the pool, pretending we were in commercials and making up skits.'

When their parents, model Gaynor Churchward and businessman-philanthropist Ronnie Driver, divorced, the sisters attended

⭐ **Schoolboy best friends toast triumph with their Oscars.**

Britain's unconventional Bedales boarding school. Minnie Driver left at sixteen and spent eight months studying languages in France before she went to drama school. By 1995 she was Trevor Eve's mistress while Juliet Stevenson plotted revenge as *The Politician's Wife* and then featured in Pierce Brosnan's first outing as James Bond in *GoldenEye*. She landed her first starring role as Benny in *Circle of Friends*, although the image projected was even more bountiful than normal – she gained thirty pounds in weight to be the hefty duckling who finds happiness with, of all people, Damon's nemesis Chris O'Donnell

By 1997's *Grosse Point Blanke* she was a familiar and popular figure with audiences and co-star John Cusak, who took much interest in his British leading lady. As Matt Damon did later that year. Love on screen is so easily transferred says Driver: 'The deeply emotional stuff can take hold of you. So many actors get involved with each other because there is this emotional overlapping. It's an occupational hazard, the hot-house environment in which those larger-than-life romances flourish.'

Especially if you're Minnie Driver. Gus Van Sant enthuses: 'We chose her because she is so realistic. Minnie has the amazing ability to make the words on the page her own. That was difficult in *Good Will Hunting* because her dialogue was less fully realized than that of the male characters. And she never flubbed a line. That's rare. Minnie has the mesmerizing presence of 1940s actresses and the subtlety and emotional range of French actresses.'

For Matt Damon, still living like the unemployed actor he had been for so long, Minnie Driver was an enchantress. 'I fell for her the minute she came in for the audition. I asked her to go out with me soon afterwards. I'm working really hard

⭐ **Actress girlfriends, Gwyneth Paltrow and Minnie Driver.**

but I don't want to sacrifice what I have with Minnie. She's awesome. She's the most wonderful woman in the world and I couldn't imagine being without her.'

He took her home to spend the American Thanksgiving holiday with his family in Boston. She in turn said before their romance collapsed: 'Matt is a fine person and that will define his success. He's also a fine actor. It's not about being a celebrity.' They were so smitten they had difficulty keeping themselves apart during the Cartier Polo finals at Windsor in the summer of 1997, but only months later he was publicly dumping her in front

of millions of strangers on *Oprah*.

He has not been forthcoming about why he ended their romance other than to say: 'It's difficult to keep personal commitment going when your career takes off. It's tough but we all have to make sacrifices and we're still good friends.'

Not as far as Minnie is concerned. How did she take to being ditched on *Oprah*?

She says with decorum: 'Most unfortunate. But, you know, boys – and I do mean "boy" – are a law unto themselves. There's absolutely no point in sitting around feeling sorry for yourself.

'The great power you have is to let it go and allow it just to be their shit. You focus on what you have, not that which has been meanly or unkindly removed. The worst thing is feeling: "How could I have so misjudged?"

'Everything has to be made so mythic. There are those archetypes that everybody has to take apart – I had to be the victim. It's horrendous breaking up with someone anyway, but to have it be so public and to be cast in a role I would never play if they were paying me – this wronged woman!

'It is unfortunate that Matt went on *Oprah*. It seemed like a good forum for him to announce to the world that we were no longer together which I found fantastically inappropriate. Of course, he was busy declaring his love for me on David Letterman's chat show a month previously.'

It was a strange, at times surreal, time for Minnie Driver and Matt Damon. By the summer of 1998 she had separated from boyfriend Taylor Hawkins, the drummer with the group Foo Fighters, and was being seen in the movie *The Governess*. Both their stars were soaring but she was philosophical about Hollywood when she talked there: 'I haven't lost myself in the unreality of the movie business – not yet anyway. I've only been part of the wake of someone else's time. But it has made me realize how far you can go from yourself and how much it is encouraged in this town. People always want you to behave like a movie star so you can carry on in the emperor's new clothes.'

One of the more bizarre of the Minnie Driver/Matt Damon encounters following the end of their affair was at the ShoWest Convention in Las Vegas, when the cinema owners of America anoint the players they believe will make them money in the future. She was 'ShoWest Female Star of Tomorrow', he was 'ShoWest Male Star of Tomorrow'. She recalled:

'It was pretty strange being the counterpart to the person you used to be with – the male and female equivalent of each other you're standing on stage with someone who is not even speaking to you anymore. That was pretty bizarre. There had to be some reality check there. It was weird, uncomfortable, sad and strange. I really wanted to enjoy it more than I did.'

Thrown together by success, their inter-mingled lives got even more complicated. And difficult.

Her bitterness shadowed the success of *Good Will Hunting*, which even against the enormous wave of applause and audience appreciation for *Titanic* and Leonardo DiCaprio was rattling up its own critical and box office success. The movie was nominated for a clutch of the annual Golden Globe Awards with the winners to be announced at the always glittering and surprising ceremony at the Beverly Hilton Hotel in Beverly Hills. The 'Globes' are a more informal, more fun affair, than the more prestigious Oscars, but nevertheless a pivotal part of Hollywood's awards season, the annual cavalcade of self-acclaim.

Good Will Hunting was nominated as Best Drama, Damon as Best Actor, Robin Williams for Best Supporting Actor and Damon and Ben Affleck for Best Screenplay. The two screenwriters wore matching smiles as they wandered through the pre-ceremony drinks gathering and dinner and found their table. 'I've got a better seat than Jack Nicholson,' laughed Damon about his idol and fellow nominee for *As Good As It Gets*. The opposition was strong, for as well as the Nicholson film they were up against *L.A. Confidential*, *The Full*

'I'm working really hard but I don't want to sacrifice what I have with Minnie. She's awesome.'

Oscar and Minnie

Monty and the apparently unbeatable if sinkable *Titanic*.

The two friends gasped as they were named as the winners of the Globe for Best Screenplay.

There was almost as much excitement at the parties afterwards. Especially the Miramax function which brought Damon and Minnie Driver together in the same room for the first time since he appeared on *Oprah*. As the Latin music kept the crowd toe-tapping and enjoying the spicy Brazilian food it was Ben Affleck who turned up first – turning heads with his date Gwyneth Paltrow, oh-so-recently split-up from Brad Pitt. Matt Damon appeared to be alone – and then he was with *Titanic* star Kate Winslet who gave him a kiss, a hug and her phone number. She wasn't gone for a moment when Winona Ryder turned up by Damon's side and all became clear to the gossips. This was a lady who mattered for Matt Damon.

Meanwhile, Minnie Driver enchanted the room in a stunning, plunging, tight-fitting evening gown. She arrived with Friends star Matt LeBlanc but on seeing Damon turned and left the room. Only minutes later she was back at the bar – just four feet away from her former lover – and doing a samba with some girlfriends. It was another very public display to the end of their affair. There would soon be another. At the Oscars, in front of a celebrity audience – and one billion television viewers.

On 10 February 1998, Matt Damon's morning was filled with phone calls congratulating him that *Good Will Hunting* had been nominated for nine Academy Awards. It was up for Best Picture, Best Actor (Damon), Best Supporting Actor (Robin Williams), Best Supporting Actress (Minnie Driver), Best Director (Gus Van Sant), Best Screenplay (written directly for the screen, Matt Damon and Ben Affleck), Best Original Dramatic Score (Danny Elfman), Best Original Song ('Miss Misery' by Elliott Smith) and Best Film Editing.

It was all getting too much like a fairytale for Matt Damon. His Best Actor fellow nominees were Jack Nicholson, Robert Duvall, Dustin Hoffman and Peter Fonda – a posse that had almost as many Academy Award nominations as Matt Damon's age. It was Robin Williams fourth Oscar nod.

It was most surely the first for Damon and Affleck who said: 'This is so beyond anything we could have wanted.'

For Minnie Driver her Best Supporting Actress nomination was gratifying but not just for her validation as an actress. She had watched from the sidelines as Damon's affair with Winona Ryder flourished and, her friends said, she had ambitions for Oscar night, 23 March 1998. Before the ceremonies a friend said: 'The main reason she wants to win is so that she can stand up in front of Winona and wave the Oscar at her. She has suffered agonies of nerves in anticipation of the Oscars.'

Two nights before the Oscars Minnie and her family walked out of a pre-Oscars party in Santa Monica after they spotted Damon. On Oscar night they were even no-shows at a Miramax party which was attended by Damon, and Winona Ryder. Damon was telling everyone who would listen that he was 'madly in love with Winona'.

But at the Oscars proper, at the Shrine Auditorium, she was very much present in that red Halston gown and red-dyed faux fox stole.

The Damon–Driver personal drama of the evening was heightened by the Oscar planners. They seated the actress and her mother and father – and his current wife Misty – and sister Kate just two rows behind Matt Damon and Ben Affleck, both attending with their mothers. ('When Moms is asking for the ticket you have to give it to her', said Affleck.)

When the *Good Will Hunting* wins were announced the TV cameras picked up no reaction from Minnie Driver. She seemed totally unmoved by it all – and her lack of animation made most Oscar reports the next day, despite the cleaning up achieved by *Titanic*.

Robin Williams took a 13–inch-tall gold-plated statuette home. In his thank-you speech Robin Williams said: 'This may be the one time when I'm

⭐ **Rented tuxedoes, permanent acclaim.**

speechless.' He wasn't, quipping, 'Thank you Matt and Ben. I still want to see some I.D.' Of Matt Damon, he said later: 'He makes fun of his good fortune – he's going to do great.'

And there was no doubting whom everyone believed the biggest thanks for the success of *Good Will Hunting* should go to: the two writers who had worked for years on their story. Damon and Affleck took away the Oscar for Best Screenplay.

At the L Street Tavern in Boston their old friends were watching and celebrating. Damon and Affleck wished them a good time with Affleck telling television cameras: 'This round's on Matt.' A grandly smiling Damon jumped in with, 'Yeah, this round's on me. Send me that bill!!'

Ben Affleck said: 'On the night of the Awards I just carried the Oscar around waist-high. I never had so many women ask me "Can I touch it?" in my life. Sadly, they were talking about the statuette.' It was all something of a fantasy on Oscar night but it was a true Cinderfella story: two struggling actors work for years on autobiographical material, craft it into a script for a film which makes $130 million dollars at the US box office and become the youngest writing team to win the Academy Award for Best Original Screenplay.

Later, a little more reflectively, Matt Damon said: 'We never thought we would actually go through the Hollywood channels much less win the Academy Awards, for God's sake. This is unbelievable.'

But true.

Chapter 7

Soldier Superstar

'I'm proud of Matt for handling stardom like such a gentleman. He's a shining example of how nice guys can finish first.'

Steven Spielberg, 1998

Matt Damon thought that life could not get much sweeter. He was a Hollywood star actor, an Oscar-winning screenwriter and the boyfriend of Winona Ryder, one of the world's most admired leading ladies.

Then he met Steven Spielberg and it all began to become even more magnificent. Spielberg was filming his moving slave ship drama *Amistad* in Boston while Damon was at work there on *Good Will Hunting*. The director's friend Robin Williams wanted to visit him. Damon recounted: 'Robin went over to see Steven and dragged me along. Steven had seen me in *Courage Under Fire* but thought I was still that skinny. A week later I got "Private Ryan".'

'Tom Hanks is the movie's star and he and his handpicked group are sent to save me because of political considerations and it raises questions like: "Is this one guy worth all these guys going after him?" My character comes to symbolize hope for everyone going home.'

In essence it is a simple story: a mother is about to be told that three of her sons have been killed in action in the Second World War within seventy-two hours, one fighting the Japanese, two separately in Europe. Her fourth son, Damon's Private Ryan, is trapped behind enemy lines. Hanks, as Captain John Miller, in a performance which will possibly give him his third Best Actor Oscar, and what's left of his platoon after D-Day, are sent to rescue Private Ryan.

'We are pissed off', says Hanks over coffee in a Californian hotel thousands of miles from Hatfield, Hertfordshire, where much of the movie was filmed and decades on from the conflict which changed the world. 'We have just gone through Hell and now we must risk our lives again. It would not be right in this movie to wrap the story in an attractive bow so everyone could understand what it meant. The film had to be ambiguous and it had to be frustrating.'

In the harrowing tradition of 1957's *Paths of Glory* and 1930's *All Quiet on the Western Front*,

✪ Pack drill for probably the most important war movie ever filmed.

both of which focused on the horrors of the First World War, Spielberg's epic *Saving Private Ryan* is one of the great anti-war movies; it is not so much an entertaining as a thought-provoking and un-settling film. Spielberg has been asked many times about it being an anti-war film and his answer remains oblique: 'I think it's an anti-war film only in that if you want to go to war after seeing this picture then it's not an anti-war film.'

'I didn't want to make a slick World War Two movie. War is horror.'

After a very short introduction set in present-day times, the film zooms onto Omaha Beach on D-Day, 6 June 1944. The audience joins the men on a landing craft as the engines, the sea and the terror all grind together. Before men's feet touch land they are separated from their bodies as blood and guts are seen spraying everywhere. This is almost war as it was and Spielberg's unrelenting first twenty-five minutes of *Saving Private Ryan* is worthy of a shelf-full of Oscars in itself.

Honours, as they were with *Schindler's List*, are incidental to him. 'There was carnage and chaos at Omaha Beach. That sequence is my attempt to portray the landing as honestly as I could. It's not just the carnage, the leg off here, the arm off there. It's the cumulative effect of shaky hand-held camera, the uncoated lenses, the desaturated colour, which makes you feel that it's fifty years ago. Nothing blurs: when you see an explosion you see every grain of sand. It's an accumulation of sounds and sights. The idea was to make it seem the film had been shot under the situation it is showing.

'In World War Two, Hollywood made films to reinvigorate, not distress, the home front. It tried to show no sacrifice was in vain, and made John Waynes out of secondary characters to sell war bonds. Those movies were not allowed to honestly portray combat. And the stills of combat camera-men were censored by the US Office of Information.

✪ **Saving Private Ryan trio – Tom Hanks, Matt Damon and Ed Burns.**

'I wanted to bring the fresh eye of the combat cameraman, not someone with preconceived notions of combat. It helps the authenticity. In recreating combat footage, hand-held cameras heighten the drama. We even threw a camera upside down to convey a cameraman dropping it, then having the courage to leave his foxhole and pick it up.

'The controversy of this film is: What price freedom? Will saving Ryan end the war sooner or just boost morale on the home front?'

For Matt Damon his character is a symbol: 'He stands for everybody's brother, for everyone getting a chance to go home. He's neutral but he represents all those other people. His character is more important than his characteristics.'

Damon points to it being Tom Hanks' film and he says he learned much watching maturity at work. On and off screen. Indeed the film establishes

✪ **Tom Hanks – the 'new' John Wayne – leads the landing in *Saving Private Ryan*.**

Tom Hanks as a heavyweight star – in every sense – and he takes the rest of the cast into the same exalted company. The making of the film made grown-ups of most of the people involved.

For Hanks, who is so liked by Hollywood (because his films make lots of money) and audiences (because usually he makes them laugh or cry), it is a dramatic departure. He is a soldier, a leader of men who is afraid to admit fear, or fallibility: 'It's a massive experience going to war. No wonder so many of the World War Two generation can't talk about it. My character Miller talks about losing people under his command but he may also be counting the people he has killed knowing lots of them are kids of eighteen or nineteen.'

As always, Hanks is believable. Damon, a life-long fan, who recalls even his early television performances – was in some awe. There's a scene well into *Joe Versus the Volcano* where Hanks, as the average guy of the title, is all but lost at sea floating atop some ridiculously expensive Vuitton-style luggage. The love of his life may or may not be

'The controversy of this film is: **What price freedom?** Will saving Ryan end the war sooner or just boost morale on the home front?'

wiped out. She lies unconscious near by. Hanks's Joe Banks fiddles with his short-wave radio and something bouncy from around Motown bursts out.

Joe in his designer and over-long shorts begins to boogie. Out in the middle of the ocean, floating on luggage, the movie's hero is getting down. Disney wouldn't try it with cartoons. But, for a moment, you believe it. And that is the magic of Tom Hanks. There's no actor to mind who could pull off that one. Or being in love with a mermaid (*Splash*, 1984) or being a thirteen-year-old boy in a thirty-five-year-old man's body (*Big*, 1988). His vulnerability works wonders.

It brought him his second Oscar in 1994 for *Forrest Gump*, which is the unlikely tale of an idiot savant with an IQ of 75 who, buffeted by fate and coincidence, leads a charmed life. Hanks also won as Best Actor in 1993 for his often moving turn as a lawyer dying of AIDS in *Philadelphia*. An Academy Award hat-trick seems likely following *Private Ryan*.

He is picture-passport perfect. At 6ft tall with dark hair and no distinguishing marks he calls himself 'a neutral point of view' for any project but insists: 'I'm not a chameleon. I don't disappear. I don't know if it's governed by my body more than anything else. I don't know if it's my butt or my nose. I don't think I'm ugly but I don't have those chiselled good looks.

'That makes me something of a blank canvas for whatever the texture of the movie. I'm lucky. I've been labelled this Everyman. So, I guess I am appropriate for Everything.

'No one fears me when my face appears on camera. I don't carry any sort of agenda with me. I used to be a wiseass but I'm not so much of a wiseass anymore. And because of all that I think the audience may be willing to go down whatever road my movies take. I don't threaten any man's sense of virility or any woman's sense of security or decorum. We're always toying with being caught in the big lie. Some moviegoers may say: "These people are faking it." Well, exactly. We're paid to pretend. It's very scary but great fun.'

In director Ron Howard's 1995 film *Apollo 13* Hanks put on a NASA spacesuit in what was to be another fabulously successful film for him, as astronaut Jim Lovell. Two days into the Apollo 13 mission in April 1970, which was to have been the third moon-walking voyage, one of two oxygen tanks blew and the main rocket engine was destroyed. For four days the world watched as Mission Control in Houston, Texas, struggled to get men and craft back alive. The astronauts did not know if they would suffocate from their own carbon dioxide, freeze or burn up on re-entry into the Earth's atmosphere.

Hanks brought the fear and courage of Lovell to the big screen; depicting the nice guy's response to an extreme situation in much the same way as Damon would as *Private Ryan*.

The younger actor thought much about the conflict he was about to help re-enact in *Private Ryan*. He talked about his thoughts: 'My generation is certainly more cynical – we are the children of the Vietnam War and I think America, in general, was younger and more idealistic back in the time of World War Two. There are stories of

Soldier Superstar

Jimmy Stewart eating bananas and milk so that he could put on weight so that he could get into the war because he was so skinny. I don't think there are many examples of that around anymore.

'For the Gulf War they never had to get beyond their reserves but it would have been interesting to see what would have happened if they had and what the reaction of my generation would be. I think that Vietnam probably made cynics out of a lot of people, the people who said: "We don't necessarily want to go to war unless we are totally positive that we're doing the right thing."

And I think World War Two has always been seen as the good war – we went there to fight the Nazis and so I think everybody can kind of get behind that whereas wars today are a little less black and white.'

Spielberg says that the 'kernel of truth around which this morality play is fictionalized' was inspired by real people. He had suffered source problems with *Amistad* – accusations that he had stolen characters from a 1989 novel – and called in eminent historian Stephen Ambrose to, in effect, vet *Saving Private Ryan*. Professor Ambrose, the Boyd Professor of History at the University of New Orleans, had a severe reaction to the film.

After seeing the first combat sequences, where thousands of Allied soldiers die coming ashore under enemy fire, Ambrose asked the projectionist to stop the film until he could compose himself.

Any fears that such a reaction would so turn off audiences that the box office would be severely handicapped were convincingly dispelled when *Private Ryan* opened in America on 24 July 1998. It earned more than $30 million in its first weekend, claiming the number one spot. By comparison the hugely successful *Forrest Gump* which also starred Tom Hanks opened in July 1994, with a weekend box office of $24.4 million. Worldwide, Paramount Studios reported, the movie's reception was 'phenomenal'.

Saving Private Ryan is fiction but the real

⭐ **Hanks and Matt with the platoon in the rubble.**

'It was more a matter of instilling in the cast the self-reliance that people had in the Forties, because **life then wasn't easy.'**

stories are never far away. Kelly Sullivan Loughren, in 1998 a twenty-seven-year-old school teacher in Cedar Falls, Iowa, has been aware of her family's Second World War story since she was a small child. 'You know, I can't remember when my parents told me,' says Loughren, a slim, red-haired woman. 'I just always knew.' In her family room of the home she is surrounded by Sullivan memorabilia: photographs, history books, a framed letter from a Navy admiral. On the wall behind her is a vintage recruiting poster of her grandfather Albert Sullivan and his older brothers, George, Francis, Joseph and Madison.

The Sullivans, then aged twenty to twenty-seven, joined the Navy in December 1941 and, against recommendations, insisted on serving on the same ship. On 13 November 1942, during the battle of Guadalcanal, their vessel, the *USS Juneau*, was hit by a Japanese torpedo.

News travelled slowly in wartime. Two months later, the Sullivans' mother, Alleta (Loughren's great-grandmother) awoke to find her living room in Waterloo, Iowa, filled with family and three naval officers, who stood when Mrs Sullivan entered the room. 'I have some news about your boys', one of the officers began, and Thomas Sullivan, the boys' father, asked, 'Which one?' The answer: 'All of them.'

The family would later learn that while four of the brothers died instantly with 550 other crewmen, the oldest, George, was thrown into the water with 140 other survivors of the initial explosion. By the time rescuers arrived, more than a week later, all but ten sailors, floating on life rafts and debris, had died of exposure or in shark attacks. George had spent four days calling for his brothers before deciding in delirium to swim off into the shark-infested water.

The Sullivans' tragedy became a brutal illustration of the real meaning of sacrifice. 'You and your husband have given a lesson in great courage to the whole country,' wrote first lady Eleanor Roosevelt in a condolence letter that was later published in newspapers. Back in Waterloo, the family coped with its grief and shock in different ways. Alleta Sullivan, eager to believe that her sons did not die in vain, helped the Navy promote sales of war bonds; her husband made public appearances with his wife but privately was drinking heavily. The boys' sister, Genevieve, then twenty-six, joined the WAVES for the rest of the war. Only Albert's young widow, Katherine, remained in seclusion. After she remarried several years later, she refused interviews out of respect for her second husband.

The Navy, understanding the inspirational power of the Sullivan story, decided in 1943 to name one of its destroyers the *USS The Sullivans* and asked Alleta Sullivan to christen it. The brothers' lives were dramatized in the film *The Sullivans*, also known as *The Fighting Sullivans*, in 1944.

The Sullivans are mentioned once in *Saving Private Ryan*, in a scene that explains the Army's morale-building plan to rescue the last surviving Ryan brother. From then on, the film draws upon the experiences of the Niland brothers of Tonawanda, New York, whose parents learned in the summer of 1944 that two of their sons, Preston and Robert, had died on D-Day and that their oldest son, Edward, was missing in action and presumed dead in the Pacific.

Meanwhile, the youngest Niland boy, Frederick, a paratrooper, was fighting somewhere in Northern France. The Army immediately organized a search for Frederick, retrieved him and sent him back home to the US to complete his service. Nearly a year later, the family got the news that Edward, whose plane had been shot down over Burma, was in fact alive in a Japanese POW camp. 'He was the last one off the plane,' says Diana Sollars, Edward's widow. 'After he parachuted out, he wandered around the jungle for three days before he was captured.' Sollars says her husband rarely spoke of his imprisonment.

Screenwriter Robert Rodat began writing *Saving Private Ryan* after he had read several books published to mark the fiftieth anniversary of D-Day. The idea of wartime sacrifice was emphasized to him by a war monument inscribed with the names of brothers who had fought and died together.

Before filming began in Hertfordshire all the principal actors underwent a six-day training session run by Captain Dale Dye, the movie's senior military adviser. Dye, who earned three Purple Hearts in Vietnam, was a technical adviser for Oliver Stone's *Platoon* (1986). 'An infantryman had a rifle and a bayonet and not much else,' says Dye. 'He had to get nose to nose with the enemy. At Normandy, it was a meat grinder, more about survival than it was about tactics. It was more a matter of instilling in the cast the self-reliance that people had in the Forties, because life then wasn't easy.' The actors were not prepared for the physical and emotional toll of boot camp and verbal abuse from a man who called all the actors 'turd'.

'Dye wears strings around his wrist, a string for each soldier that died under his command,' said squad member Vin Diesel: 'On the last day of boot camp, he said, "You give me a chance to pay back these men that died, you redeem their lives." And

✪ **Full blast ahead for the troops in Steven Spielberg's award-winning *Saving Private Ryan*.**

Matt Damon

we were in tears. When you have somebody open up like that, you take it very seriously.'

Professor Ambrose calls the film 'the best war movie ever made', pointing out that in real life and in the film wounded men, disembowelled by mortar fire, die in agony, crying for their mothers, for water, for morphine. 'I wouldn't have dreamed that anyone could make a movie that recreated Omaha Beach,' he said. 'The guys who were there are going to see this and have to hide their eyes.'

Ambrose's reaction is endorsed by the actors who said they found it difficult to shake off the experience. After shooting was completed last fall, Edward Burns visited the Second World War cemeteries near Omaha Beach, where 117,153 servicemen are buried. He recalled: 'I'm not an emotional guy but the film had a profound effect on me, seeing all the graves of guys that were five or eight years younger than me, who died horrible deaths. These were different men than our generation.' When Burns went inside the cemetery's small chapel, he began to cry uncontrollably. 'I got a chill down my spine. To this day I have no idea what was going on. Guys my age, we sort of live this extended adolescence. These men were forced to grow up. I think it was a real slap in the face.'

Burns said that for all the actors filming and the aftermath had been traumatic: 'It was easily the worst experience of my life. Physically exhausting. It dropped to about forty-five degrees at night. You'd get rained on all day doing your six-mile hikes and your night manoeuvres and your cleaning and loading of weapons. And you'd come back to the fire and just try to dry your uniform as best you could. And then you'd get your three hours of sleep. And it just wasn't worth it to try to take this uniform off because you'd only have to put the cold, wet uniform on in the morning.'

Filming went on around the south-eastern coast of Ireland, recreating the invasion of Normandy, during which the weather resembled

✪ 'No, Sir.' Matt, as Private Ryan, balks at orders from Officer Tom Hanks.

⭐ **The tears of war.**

that of the real D-Day with cold, blustery, heavy seas.

'Movie actors tend to be awfully spoiled,' said Spielberg adding, 'There are masseuses, trainers, trailers, take-out, you name it. The perks are pretty amazing, and not just for the movie stars but for up-and-coming actors as well. This movie was not going to be for the perkaholic. I'm not a Method director. I don't believe in making anybody suffer for their art. But in this case, I thought that all of us had to feel some pain.'

All the actors did in some way. They were carefully picked by Spielberg, an independent bunch, some of whom have directed their own movies: Edward Burns, Vin Diesel, Barry Pepper, Tom Sizemore, Jeremy Davies, Adam Goldberg, Giovanni Ribisi and Matt Damon.

'When I cast Matt, he was a complete unknown,' says Spielberg. 'Then, of course, he came out of hiding with *Good Will Hunting* and overnight became a movie star. It's good for our movie.'

But Damon didn't attend boot camp. 'They'd been wading through mud puddles and sleeping face down in water and here I show up all prim and proper and ready to go. They were, like, "Why the hell did this kid not have to come to boot camp? Who the fuck is he?" '

The reaction was understandable. After a couple of days and nights of boot camp some of the actors decided they had had enough. In addition to sleep deprivation, they were suffering from sprained ankles, bronchitis, bouts of vomiting. They wanted to have something left for Spielberg and the movie. The only one at ease was Hanks. 'He was Forrest Gump,' said Adam

Goldberg adding: 'It was frightening. I'd be running alongside him and be seriously doubling over, and Hanks would have his chest out and his chin up, and he'd be in fantastic stride the second mile, the third mile, the fifth mile.'

Hanks knew what he was in for when he signed on to boot camp. Unlike the other actors, he was psychologically and physically prepared for it. He also saw it as the only rehearsal time they would have: 'I was worried that there was going to be some sort of moment where we became a divided group. It would've been a drag, because you have to negotiate so much anyway as far as making a movie. We needed to be unified, even if what we're unified in is hating the experience.'

Spielberg was aware of the potential for mutiny. He says that Hanks called him in the editing room while he was cutting *Amistad* and told him that they all looked like real soldiers. The bad news was that half of them wanted to leave the film. 'I said: "Tom, You're not only the character Captain Miller and my good buddy, but you're also a director – get these guys to stay." And he said: "Okay, boss, I'll handle it." ' And he did.

Which made all involved part of one of the century's great moviemaking experiences. Spielberg, who is responsible for seven of the most successful films of all time, said: 'This is the most rewarding movie I've done aside from *Schindler's List* because it's reality.

'I really wanted to tell the stories of these men. I wanted before the end of the century to tell their experience as opposed to adding one more movie to a long train of World War Two films that were filled with excitement and adventure and sacrifice and nobility. Do you sugarcoat it by telling people that dying is easy, and dying is noble? How many movies have said that to us *ad nauseam*? I'd rather create some *nauseam*. I would rather show how these boys really died. I feel I made the movie as a memorial.'

For Matt Damon it was a growing-up experience. He had the title role and will always be associated with one of the most talked-about movies ever. He said: 'It was a great lesson. The only way I can describe Steven is this: I was on the set one day and he said: "Hey, you want to see a movie I made when I was fourteen?" He showed me this army movie, it was his first army movie. I watched that and it all made sense to me – it's simple, he's a genius.

'Literally, there were dolly shots where you think: "Wait a minute ... !!!" And he says: "Yeah, I used that in *Raiders*, I did that in *Jaws*." I tried to keep up with him one day just to see what it was like to be Steven Spielberg. So I kind of stayed two steps behind him and followed him around while he directed a day's work.

'By the end of the day I was cooked. He had this well of energy that he draws from when he needs it and he burned me out. I couldn't keep up with him. Working with him was a tremendous reward.'

As the century was drawing to a close it seemed there were nothing but rewards for the young star. Even in the city where the odds are stacked against everyone, and which, in its architectural and material excesses, brashly symbolizes the millennial American experience – Las Vegas.

'When I cast Matt, he was a complete unknown', says Spielberg. 'Then, of course, he came out of hiding with *Good Will Hunting* and overnight became a movie star. **It's good for our movie.**'

Chapter 8

Good Will Punting

'Everybody has a weakness.'

Las Vegas casino owner, Jack Binion

The sun's not been up long, but out in Glitter Gulch the temperature is one hundred degrees. Inside Binion's Horseshoe Hotel and Casino the air conditioning is having bad luck doing any more than move the tobacco fog in a gentle swirl around the giant gaming room.

'Everybody,' says Jack Binion as he squints at the crowd testing themselves and his facilities, 'has a weakness. We here in Las Vegas just give you the opportunity to run into the right one.'

Matt Damon played at the 29th Annual World Series of Poker with fellow actor Ed Norton. They were surrounded by 349 of the best card players in the world – probably the only two in the place who realized they did not have a chance at the one million dollars in prize money. 'We never once entertained the fantasy of actually winning,' said Damon.

He and Norton had poker parachutes. They got to turn the cards with these world-class gamblers as part of their research for the 1999 movie *Rounders*. Matt Damon is an altogether different lawyer than in *The Rainmaker*. He's a law student with a gift for cards who is drawn back into the game which previously bankrupted him by his sleazeball best friend Norton, who is just out of prison. After *Private Ryan* for Damon and *The People Vs Larry Flynt* for Norton, the card-sharping movie gave some relief.

'This is the first movie I've ever made where somebody doesn't get shot,' said director John Dahl. It is, he said, 'a guy movie'. And Damon and Norton are the main guys in a movie which has the netherworld, misdemeanour feel of the small hours. We've had golden boy turned to gambling before. Paul Newman was *The Hustler* and Steve McQueen *The Cincinnati Kid* in the 1960s, while Matt Dillon was *The Flamingo Kid* and Tom Cruise was seduced by *The Colour of Money* in the 1980s.

Rounders, which gets more character from actors like Martin Landau, John Malkovich and John Turturro and glamour from Gretchen Mol and Famke Janssen, was another chance for Damon to display his impressive cinema range.

Which was why he was taking the Vegas poker session so seriously. After all the movies and the Oscars and the attention, this was Matt Damon back to being Matt Damon: 'This is my first experience of being Me in public and I find it really weird that all these photographers have come. It happened at the Oscars, but that is a huge event in its own right. This is just me making a decision to come and play in the tournament.

'I suppose I recognized my life was going to change. I imagined it would be more low-key because there are such serious gamblers here. But

✪ **Looks tough at the top for Matt.**

Good Will Punting

the announcer goes "They're off" and suddenly ninety-three cameras are on me and I'm thinking: "Oh my God, don't these people realize I'm going to lose in like two minutes? That I'm just here on a lark? For God's sake, if you're going to cover a card tournament, at least cover the real players.'

World Series contestants have to put up $10,000 as an entry fee but Damon's has been covered by the organizers, starved of celebrity contestants since the death of tournament regular Telly Savalas. 'We get a couple of kids in from the movies,' drawls one unimpressed dealer of Damon and Norton, 'but all that matters is whether they know one end of an ace from another.' They do.

The actors had extensive coaching for their film which is set in New York, where high-stakes,

illegal underground poker is played. Damon's character Mike can't quite leave the gaming tables behind. Mike McGee, who was one of Britain's best hopes in the World Series, played Damon during a warm-up session. 'He's up there with the best,' says McGee. 'I knew he was the most skilful player next to me on the table, so I targeted him to knock him out of the game. And I did.'

Damon's biggest solo bet to date was a $1,000 wager he laid on the college football team in Knoxville, Tennessee, to beat rivals from Florida in a crucial match. He got to know the team during the filming of *The Rainmaker*. The bet was part-celebration, part-solidarity play, in honour of a star player who could have gone pro but stayed back a year to play with his team-mates in that particular game. 'I thought that if he lost, my $1,000 would be as nothing to his feelings of failure.' Damon had to settle for a moral victory. The team lost. 'I'm trying to make it sound noble but I was furious. I needed that money.'

He was luckier on a previous trip to Vegas with Ben Affleck: they put $100 each on '33', shirt number of former Boston Celtics basketball star Larry Bird. They also put $4,000 on black and cashed in on both bets. 'We were real broke at the time. It was just before I was making *Courage Under Fire* and we couldn't even afford to be there but by the time we left we felt rich.'

He talks of that evening with real happiness and despite the million-dollar film deals says: 'Money is still meaningful to me. I've been told I'm going to make all this money but I haven't seen any of it and my lifestyle hasn't changed. I have no home and no car and I've been from hotel to hotel for two-and-a-half years. It's debilitating because I'm somebody who needs that base.'

He also needs to stay in the movies. He dropped his last $1,000 at the tables on a pair of kings between by two paces: 'It was a real experience but obviously I need more practice. I think acting is more difficult but poker and acting are similar in that everybody thinks they can act and everybody thinks they can play poker.'

But not everyone knows they are lucky. Matt Damon and Ben Affleck knew just how well they had done. Life for them towards the end of 1998 seemed packed with good news. They were also being comforted – and counselled – by celebrity veterans.

Winona Ryder, with whom Damon bought a $2.5 million dollar Spanish-style villa in Beverly Hills not long after their Oscar partying has been in the spotlight for a decade. She was twenty-five in 1998 and her range of films had been remarkable.

As has been her influence – something Matt Damon did not fully realize when she replaced Minnie Driver in his affections. Then his new love told him her story about her experiences with movie giants, Martin Scorsese and Francis Coppola, for whom she made 1993's *Dracula*.

She co-starred with Michelle Pfeiffer and Daniel Day-Lewis in Scorsese's film adaptation of Edith Wharton's *Age of Innocence*, which the director, arguably America's best, had always wanted to make. Scorsese was coming off *Goodfellas* and Cape Fear and wanted something different, like a period drama. Winona Ryder wrote about *Age of Innocence* for her final high school English report and got an 'A'. 'I kept thinking, God, one day if they make a movie of it I want to play May Welland.' Some years later she was at a Hollywood award ceremony for Scorsese:

'He was standing with his parents and I didn't want to meet him 'cause I was way too nervous. He's just so brilliant you feel you're just the size of an ant. But this guy from Fox dragged me over to him and I just kinda stood there. He turned around and said: "Oh, I'm a great admirer of yours. What do you think of *Age of Innocence*."

'And I was like: "Ah. Well. I well, umm." I just stuttered. Someone got in front of me and I just ran away. I couldn't understand if he was offering me the part or if he was just saying he was doing the movie. Then I was sitting in my trailer (on the set of *Dracula*) and he called. I was caught off-guard but he said: "So, we're doing this and it will be fun."

'I agreed and flipped out in my trailer. But I didn't want to get real excited in front of Francis because we are very good friends and I wanted to be professional: "I'm still working on *Dracula*."

'I've been told I'm going to make all this money **but I haven't seen any of it** and my lifestyle hasn't changed.'

Good Will Punting

⭐ **Playing the odds for real at the World Poker Championships in Las Vegas.**

Inside, I was like: "I can't wait." '

For Matt Damon it was like hearing about a Hollywood *Who's Who*. And her former boyfriend was Johnny Depp (after they broke up he changed the tattoo on his right shoulder from 'Winona Forever' to 'Wino Forever') so there was acting pedigree to follow.

But strong-minded Winona found her match in Damon. They share similar backgrounds and argue over who is the biggest hippy. She wins.

She was born in Winona, Minnesota, raised mainly in an upmarket Californian 'Freestyle community' and her godfather was the late and legendary turn-on guru Timothy Leary. She hates Shakespeare. Her Bible is *Catcher in the Rye* ('I've read it fifty times') and her favourite, heavily underlined phrase from it is: 'The goddamn movies. They can ruin you.'

Her favourite writer is George Orwell and she typed-out ninety pages of one of his novels when she was eleven years old. Musically, she goes from heavy metal to the theme from *Breakfast at Tiffanys*. She's had an agent since the age of twelve and probably an opinion since the cradle. She has two brothers and a sister, a father Michael who runs a bookstore specializing in Sixties books and a mother Cindy who is a video producer. She is affectionately known as Noni and replaced her family name of Horowitz with the stage name Ryder ('My father picked it out of a hat') when she starred opposite Charlie Sheen in her first film *Lucas* (1986). In between she's worked with Tim Burton on *Beetlejuice* and *Edward Scissorhands* (with Depp), with Christian Slater on the wonderfully macabre *Heathers* and with Dennis Quaid in *Great Balls of Fire*, playing Jerry Lee Lewis's child-bride, Myra.

But she appears grounded. 'I was a really weird kid obsessed with gangster movies. You know when you're that age – maybe this is just me and

I'm a weirdo. I had really short hair and I wore these old suits and ties. On the third day at my new school I got beaten up by some boys who thought I was an effeminate boy. I wasn't upset about it. I was not the little rebel. My mind was very sweet, innocent. Every time I start to think about celebrity, what is happening to us, I try to change the subject in my head because it's not what I got into this whole thing for. I don't do things that are harmful to me.

'There are so many jaded kids now. I hate to see kids with drinks in their hands, chain-smoking just to be trendy. None of that is romantic or cool to me. I've gone to parties that just scared me, grossed me out. I see star-fuckers and people who do that stuff just to be seen. It's sick. I've already seen actors who've been destructive. I've had friends – really good friends – who as soon as they became successful went from being happy to being totally messed up. Most kids are in acting for different reasons – lots because it's a fun thing, fame and fortune, girls and boys.'

She says she and Damon and Ben and Gwyneth just want to work: 'The big influence on me was Sarah Miles. When I saw her in *Ryan's Daughter* I really wanted to be an actress. She was breathtaking. Subtle. Beautiful. She's bowled me over in everything I've seen her in.'

With her friend Gwyneth Paltrow, now happy with Ben Affleck after ending her long relationship with Brad Pitt, the group made Hollywood's hottest quartet. Affleck added to their allure as the action star with Bruce Willis of the $140 million-budgeted thriller *Armageddon* in the late summer of 1998.

But Gwyneth Paltrow was to be the girl between Matt Damon and Winona Ryder. They were going to take a long, European trip together. With the remarkable *Mr Ripley*.

⭐ **Light my fire – award-winning beauty Winona Ryder.**

Chapter 9

Riding High

'It's very bizarre being part of pop culture.'
Gwyneth Paltrow

Gwyneth Paltrow looks the part of a movie star but can be forgiven for seeking challenges in banking given that Brad Pitt and now Ben Affleck and Matt Damon are adoringly rated by glossy magazines as more beautiful than she. Her mother Blythe Danner is one of America's most respected stage actresses and her father Bruce Paltrow a hugely successful television producer, responsible for series like *St Elsewhere* and *Friends*. The young, willowy blonde actress might have been forgiven for seeking challenges in banking.

But, no, she stuck to acting and with it celebrity, first by default and now endorsed by films like the updated *Great Expectations* and the youth hit *Sliding Doors*. Moments ago she always sounded like a Truman Capote heroine murmuring 'I'm just a girl' but she is telling herself – and so is the calendar – that she is grown-up.

She turned twenty-six in September 1998 and said: 'I feel like it is a woman's age. I just mean in terms of a number because obviously everybody is different. For example, if someone said they were twenty-six, you'd know they would have to be a woman, right?'

For her generation Gwyneth Paltrow is cool; she has a crossover style which can grace the black-tie Oscar ceremonies or a pair of jeans. On film she can play a scruffball con artist (1983's *Flesh and Bone*) or the very English Emma. She is, say her

crowd, infuriatingly capable, something that was required when she began filming *The Talented Mr Ripley* with Matt Damon in the title role and Jude Law as the man they both love.

While the relationship of the two men dominates the film, it is Paltrow as Marge – to Ripley's eyes the constant gooseberry, the interference – which heightens the tingling apprehension of the movie. And Paltrow, the cool, blonde beauty is an uneasy presence, someone audiences are not quite sure about.

She and Matt Damon are the Cary Grant and Grace Kelly for a new generation, players with not just a certain smile but also a certain sophistication. While Damon raced at stardom, his co-star maintains: 'I was in no rush to be the star of a movie because there is so much responsibility placed on your shoulders. I wanted to do smaller parts, really diverse things, things that are opposite from the last role you've done.'

With all of them – Damon, Affleck, Ryder and Paltrow and their friends and co-stars – there is an extraordinary belief that it will all come good for them. Matt Damon says: 'I think I believed it could happen and I think we are a generation who believe we can make it happen.'

Paltrow admits hers is a confidence which can be traced back to her family. Once her father had

⭐ **Nothing will wipe the smile off that face.**

finally conceded that she should pursue her acting career (after she had appeared with her mother in *Picnic*), it was just a matter of waiting for the catalytic break. Enter the man in many players' lives – Steven Spielberg. He is a family friend and she was given a cameo in his 1991 *Hook* as the young Wendy (Robin Williams was Peter Pan) and her career flew from there.

Why, then, Matt Damon and Ben Affleck and Winona Ryder and Gwyneth Paltrow? Damon says he thinks about it. The others were destined, he believes. Him? Modesty forbids. Ben Affleck said: 'Matt Damon's always been a really smart, funny, interesting guy. The difference is now that every teenage girl in the world is shrieking for him. I don't think he will get too carried away by it.'

The writing partners have three screenwriting commitments. It makes them even more valuable to moviemakers. Kevin Smith, who helped them get *Good Will Hunting* produced, was paid back when the two actors agreed to star in his Dogma for way below their going rate.

'When a brother is being offered five to seven million dollars for a film and I'm paying something like eighteen hundred dollars this is a huge testimony to his loyalty and passion,' said director Smith of the film in which Damon and Affleck played angels banned from Heaven. They want back. Emma Thompson was God and the cast also included Alan Rickman, Salma Hayek, Linda Fiorentino and America's late-1990s major comic-actor sensation Chris Rock.

Damon's voice is also in demand. Fox Animation cast it in *Planet Ice* where he talks the character Cale, who is fighting to save the survivors following the destruction of Earth. The animated movie also used the star voices of Drew Barrymore and Nathan Lane and was evidence for Damon that it was not just his image but his acting that was wanted.

Matt Damon's star was so strong in 1998 that multi-million dollar projects were sometimes down to his decision. Fox Studio were about to fund $35 million for director Ang Lee's Civil War romantic epic *To Live On*, with Damon as the leading man. Lee's reputation – critical and box office – was immense, with strong films like *Sense and Sensibility* and *The Ice Storm*.

But when Damon declined the role, the money for it also vanished. The counter to that was the enthusiasm his agreement to play John Grady Cole in *All the Pretty Horses* created in Hollywood and among fans of author Cormac McCarthy's border trilogy.

McCarthy's first novel is a rites-of-passage tale about a young man growing up and surviving in the tough territory along the US–Mexican border of the late Forties. The film is anticipated as a major release in 1999 and a strong contender for the Oscars 2000.

Millennium awards or not, Matt Damon is already learning that despite the dreams that have woken into reality for him, there is still a lot to do to stay ahead of the game in Tinseltown. Hollywood is not for the meek. And it is easy to get ego all over your face. Damon has already found that out.

For their *Good Will Hunting* script, he and Ben Affleck had the counsel of many people, including Mel Gibson, who hated the title, and Hollywood master screenwriter William Goldman. Goldman has created and worked on films like *All The President's Men* and *Butch Cassidy and the Sundance Kid* and is one of the most revered of writers. He apparently had a strong relationship with the two fledgling screenwriters. They thought they were 'in' with him.

It was only four months after they had worked with him on *Good Will Hunting* that they were all by chance in the lobby of the Four Seasons Hotel in New York. Matt Damon was delighted to see such a mentor. He strode over and said, 'Mr Goldman!'

Goldman looked at Damon and replied, 'Are you my chauffeur?'

✪ **Gwyneth Paltrow, who tangles with Matt on screen in *The Talented Mr Ripley*.**

Filmography

MYSTIC PIZZA: US, 102 minutes, 1988, Samuel Goldwyn Company, Levinson/Rosenfelt Productions
Shooting Start: 12 October 1987
Locations: Mystic and Hartford, Connecticut; Rhode Island
Director: Donald Petrie
Cast: Julia Roberts, Annabeth Gish, Lili Taylor, Jojo Barboza, Vincent D'Onofrio, William R. Moses, Adam Storke, Conchata Ferrell, Matt Damon
Screenplay from story: Amy Jones

RISING SON: US, 120 minutes; 1990, Turner Network Television (TNT)
Shooting Start: 28 February 1990
Location: Atlanta, Georgia
Director: John David Coles
Cast: Brian Dennehy, Piper Laurie, Matt Damon, Jane Adams, Ving Rhames, Tate Donovan
Screenplay from story: Bill Phillips

SCHOOL TIES: US, 110 minutes, 1992, Jaffe-Lansing Productions, Paramount Pictures
Shooting Start: 3 September 1991
Location: Middlesex, Massachusetts
Director: Robert Mandel
Cast: Brendon Fraser, Chris O'Donnell, Matt Damon, Randell Batinkoff, Andrew Lowrey, Cole Hauser, Ben Affleck, Chesty Smith, Anthony Rapp, Amy Locane, Peter Donat
Screenplay from story: Dick Wolf

GERONIMO: AN AMERICAN LEGEND: US, 115 minutes, 1993, Columbia
Shooting Start: 3 May 1993
Locations: Moab, Utah Sony Pictures Studios; Culver City, California
Director: Walter Hill
Cast: Jason Patric, Gene Hackman, Robert Duvall, Wes Studi, Matt Damon, Rodney A. Grant, Kevin Tighe
Screenplay from Story: John Milius

THE GOOD OLD BOYS: US, 120 minutes, 1995 , Turner Network Television (TNT)
Shooting Start: July 1994
Director: Tommy Lee Jones
Location: New Mexico, Texas
Cast: Tommy Lee Jones, Terry Kinney, Frances McDormand, Sissy Spacek, Sam Shephard, Wilford Brimley, Walter Olkewicz, Matt Damon, Brucer McGill, Park Overall
Screenwriter: Tommy Lee Jones

GLORY DAZE: US, 104 minutes, 1996 Fusion Studios, Woodward Productions, Weiny Bro Productions
Shooting Start: 19 September 1994
Location: Los Angeles and Santa Cruz, California
Director: Rich Wilkes
Cast: Ben Affleck, Sam Rockwell, Megan Ward, French Stewart, Vien Hong, Vinnie DeRamus, Kristen Bauer, John Rhys Davies, Matt Damon
Screenplay: Rich Wilkes

COURAGE UNDER FIRE: US, 115 minutes, 1996, Fox 2000 Pictures
Shooting Start: 16 October 1995
Locations: Yuma, Arizona; Austin and El Paso, Texas
Director: Edward Zwick
Cast: Denzel Washington, Meg Ryan, Lou Diamond Phillips, Michael Moriarty, Matt Damon, Bronson Pinchot
Screennplay: Patrick Sheane Duncan

JOHN GRISHAM'S THE RAINMAKER: US, 137 minutes, 1997, Douglas/Reuther Productions
Shooting Start: 7 October 1996
Locations: Memphis, Tennessee; Alameda, California; San Francisco, California
Director: Francis Ford Coppola
Cast: Matt Damon, Claire Danes, Danny DeVito, Danny Glover, Virginia Madsen, Jon Voight, Mary Kay Place, Mickey Rourke, Roy Scheider,

Andrew Shue, Dean Stockwell, Randy Travis, Teresa Wright, Red West
Screenplay: John Grisham from his novel

CHASING AMY: US, 105 minutes, 1997, Miramax Films
Shooting start: 29 April 1996
Location: New Jersey
Director: Kevin Smith
Cast: Ben Affleck, Joey Lauren, Adams, Jason Lee, Dwight Ewell, Casey Affleck, Brian O'Halloran, Matt Damon
Screenplay: Kevin Smith

GOOD WILL HUNTING: US, 126 minutes, 1997, Miramax Films, A Band Apart
Shooting Start: 14 April 1997
Location: Boston, Massachusetts
Director: Gus Van Sant
Cast: Matt Damon, Robin Williams, Ben Affleck, Minnie Driver, S. Stellan Skarsgard, J. Casey Affleck, Cole Hauser, George Plimpton
Screenplay: Matt Damon and Ben Affleck

SAVING PRIVATE RYAN: US, 170 minutes, 1998, DreamWorks SKG, Paramount Pictures
Shooting Start: 27 June 1997
Locations: County Wexford, Ireland; Hatfield, Hertfordshire, England
Director: Steven Spielberg
Cast: Tom Hanks, Tom Sizemore, Edward Burns, Matt Damon, Jeremy Davies, Adam Goldberg
Screenplay: Frank Darabont and Robert Rodat

PLANET ICE: US, 92 minutes, 1998, Fox Family Films
Shooting Start: October 1997
Location: Fox Animation Studios, Phoenix, Arizona
Director: Art Vitello
Cast: Matt Damon, Bill Pullman, Drew Barrymore, Nathan Lane
Screenplay: Ben Edlund

ROUNDERS: US, 125 minutes, 1998, Spanky Pictures, Miramax Films
Shooting Start: 15 December 1997
Location: New York City, New York
Director: John Dahl
Cast: Matt Damon, Edward Norton, Gretchen Mol, John Turturro, John Malkovich, Martin Landau, Melina Kanakaredes, Famke Janssen
Screenplay: David Levien

DOGMA: US, 1999, Miramax Films, View Askew
Shooting Start: 16 March 1998
Location: Pittsburgh, Pennsylvania Red Bank, New Jersey
Director: Kevin Smith
Cast: Ben Affleck, Matt Damon, Linda Fiorentino, Salma Hayek, Chris Rock, Alan Rickman, Kevin Smith
Screenplay: Kevin Smith

THE TALENTED MR RIPLEY: US, 1999, Mirage Enterprises
Shooting Start: July 1998
Locations: Rome, Venice and Naples, Italy
Director: Anthony Minghella
Cast: Matt Damon, Gwyneth Paltrow, Jude Law
Screenplay: Anthony Minghella from *The Talented Mr Ripley* by Patricia Highsmith

Matt Damon can be contacted at:

Creative Artists Agency,
9830 Wilshire Boulevard,
Beverly Hills,
California 90212
USA

Filmography

⭐ Matt alongside co-star Robert Duvall in
Walter Hill's *Geronimo: An American Legend.*

Picture research: Lois Linden, Hollywood.
Picture credits:
Hubert Boesl & Kurt Krieger @ Famous
Douglas Thompson Film Archive
Associated Press
Paramount Pictures
20th Century Fox
Miramax Films
Turner Pictures
Columbia Pictures